Walking in Balance

ᎢᎦᏗᏍᎭᏊ ᎾᎿᎢ ᎡᏙᎲᎢ

gatihaquu nahnai edohvi

By Abraham Bearpaw

Contents

Contents

Contents *(Continued)*

ISBN-13: 9798365907287

Imprint: Independently published

Walking In Balance

ᎢᎦᏗᎭᏊ ᎾᏏᎢ ᎡᏙᎯᎢ - Igatihaquu nahnai edohvi

What does fulfillment mean to you? When you close your eyes and picture what it looks like for you to be fulfilled, what do you see? Are you with others? Are you happy? If you can visualize where you want to be then the Walking In Balance curriculum can help you get there. What lies herein is a guide to living a fulfilled life of wellness. A guide that has been passed down since time immemorial by our ancestors. I call the curriculum or collection of teachings Walking In Balance. Appropriately named I think because that has long been the ambition of our people. I say our people because we are all related and we are all connected.

I hear it said often that "you can't have it all". Says who? I often wonder. The people who say you can't do something are usually just too afraid to try themselves and that's okay. Some of us are not ready to heal and everyone's journey is sacred and different for a reason. However, if you are ready for a change then keep reading and I will tell you about how I and others have begun to heal through the simple teachings of the Walking In Balance curriculum.

The Walking In Balance components are derived from Cherokee cultural teachings that have been passed down since time immemorial. These teachings that promote wellness and balance are not exclusive to Cherokees as many Native people have similar teachings. However, I feel that these teachings should be shared because they can benefit us all and sharing is a Native value as well. I have been teaching the Walking In Balance curriculum for years but have not transcribed all of the teachings together until now. Even though Cherokee people have our own syllabary, many of our cultural teachings continue to be passed down orally, which means not everyone has access to this information. So, I decided to write down this program for living a well and balanced life so that it can be shared by everyone. One of the teachings in Cherokee culture is that nobody should tell another how they should live their life. So, I hope I do not leave you with the impression that you should do these things or have to do these things. However, I know from experience that it is challenging to live well if you do not know how. So, I am writing this for those who are searching for ways to improve their situations and live a fulfilled life of wellness. I will outline how the Walking In Balance teachings have improved my life and it is my hope that they do the same for you.

I wanted to write this book for those who are looking for simple solutions to improve symptoms of anxiety, chronic stress and frustration. However, this information can be helpful to anyone who wants to live a fulfilled and balanced life of wellness. Do you find yourself living with anxiety, frustration or struggle with self-belief? Have you grown tired of disliking your body, personality or living situation? I have and I work every day to make sure that I show love and acceptance to the person in the mirror. By following the teachings of the Walking In Balance program, I have greatly improved my situation and I live a happy and fulfilled life of wellness. Granted, I do not regularly break out in song with forest creatures but I am happy nonetheless. I have struggled with anxiety my entire life due to childhood trauma and other issues and am happy to have finally found success but I have to do the work. I was given these teachings when I was young and they helped me find relief but I did not practice them regularly enough to protect me from developing negative coping skills throughout the years. However, I am happy to say that I now practice these principles daily and I live a much more balanced and peaceful life.

I am blessed to have benefitted from many teachers throughout the years and I have had many opportunities to learn new ways of thinking and doing but I struggled at times to find sustained success. Looking back now, I realize that when I did find something that worked for me I would only do it long enough to feel better and then I would stop. So, all of the time and energy that was put into me at ceremonial grounds, rehabilitation centers and emotional growth schools was under-utilized because I had no patience for the process. As I mentioned before, I was given this information when I was young and it helped me tremendously.

However, throughout the years in my travels all over the country, these teachings gave way to those of the dominant society.

I began to view these teachings as less important and my practice of them waned. That was my first mistake. Next, I began to self-medicate because I did not feel well since I was out of balance with myself, my spirit and my environment. And so began many years spent in frustration and anger at everything. Thankfully, I was able to quit the substance abuse cycle and I have been sober now for many years. However, once I got sober all of my problems didn't go away but were amplified because I no longer dulled my senses with alcohol. I realized early on in sobriety that I needed to augment my sobriety program with a total program for living to find true fulfillment and sustain the progress that I had made. This program is not intended to replace any recovery or mental health program but instead can supplement them. I work a recovery program, go to therapy regularly and the Walking In Balance program has helped me tremendously with both endeavors.

In order to secure my future I realized that I had to kick it old-school. Go back to basics. The program's origins came about when I was thinking about the teachings that my ancestors followed and tried to convey to me. I thought about the sacrifices that they had made so that our cultural and spiritual teachings were perpetuated. The strength and perseverance they showed in times of hardship amazed me. Then I looked in the mirror and I saw anxiety and fear and I started to wonder about the disconnection between previous generations and mine. Our loss of cultural connection, in some cases, meant that we also lost many of the positive coping skills that were embedded into our daily living. Many of us also continue to heal from historical trauma as well. I began to realize that I had lost my connection with the wellness teachings that are found in our culture and this meant that I was no longer connected to my spirit, to those around me, or to my environment. However, I was relieved because I knew the way back home.

Throughout the years these cultural teachings have helped me navigate some perilous situations and I was happy to find that once again my ancestors were there for me. It didn't take long to formulate a remedy for what ailed me. Gratitude, Mindfulness, Self-Compassion, Wellness, Sobriety, Respect, Communication, Self-Care, Perseverance, Service, Balance and Action. When I looked back at everything that I was taught through our ceremonial ways it was these cultural teachings that called out to me. So, I began to put this Indigenous knowledge into practice again and all these years later I am still sober and I find I wake up every day happy to be me and excited about life.

Admittedly, I struggled in the beginning to implement these teachings into my daily living because I happened to live in California at the time and was not near where any Cherokee ceremonies are held. Then I remembered two other Cherokee cultural teachings that helped me to put everything together. Flexibility and adaptability. These two values have enabled our people to survive and thrive despite any adversity we have faced. So, until I could be immersed once again in Cherokee culture and ceremonial ways I found ways to practice each of these components where I was. Cherokee people still have the same beliefs and values but we can be flexible in how we practice these teachings and adapt to changes in our society. Gratitude was taught when hunting and gathering but I can still be grateful to go to the grocery store or when I sit down for a meal with my family.

I have since moved back to the Cherokee Nation because I believe it is one of my spiritual purposes to give others access to these teachings to help them cope with life's changes. I have taught this program many times now for several organizations and the results have been extremely positive. These teachings were traditionally perpetuated through various cultural practices such as ceremonies, games, hunting and gathering, art and other activities. However, even though our society continues to change we can continue to practice these teachings by different means.

Though it may look like a lot of information to take in at once, the program is pretty simple and involves very small changes to your daily living. Throughout the book, you will see how each of the components has changed my life for the better. The program will enhance protective factors and enable you to cope when life's challenges inevitably come your way. Practicing this program has helped me not just in everyday life but when traumatic events happen in my life as well. Instead of focusing on any losses I instead can catch my negative thoughts and change them to positive thoughts that focus on being grateful. This has allowed me to cope more positively and has brought peace and balance to my life. Throughout the book, I will outline how each pillar of the program helps you to Walk In Balance and I will also suggest ways to implement them into your busy schedules. However, the beauty of the program is that you can tailor it to your specific needs and you can practice the components in your own way. You will find that some components have the same action steps and that is because some coping skills actually help you in different areas. My hope is that by the end of the book you will have a clear picture of how the Walking In Balance program can improve your life and have concrete action steps to take to make it happen.

Introduction- Ancestral Teachings

I was very young when my uncle Jim Mankiller began to teach me what Walking In Balance was all about. One day, we were at our ceremonial grounds which we call Stomp Grounds because the Stomp Dance is an important part of our ceremonial life. While there my uncle pointed at the posts that marked the entrance to the grounds. "You see those posts there?" he said. "Once you pass those posts you no longer have enemies. All of your anger and resentment, you have to leave it outside those posts." So, I did as I was instructed and every time I went to the grounds I would leave all of my negativity outside the posts. I was also taught to practice self-compassion by forgiving others and I remember how free I felt without all of that negative stuff weighing me down. That was the first time that I knew it was possible to live at one with my spirit. However, the feeling was often fleeting because when the ceremony was over and I left the grounds I would once again be encumbered by anxiety, fear and resentment. I remember wishing that I could feel good about myself all of the time but it would be a while before I would be able to accomplish that goal.

For Cherokee people, balance is the foundation of our culture and ceremonies. We are taught to live in balance with our spirit and our environment because Cherokee people have long recognized the connection between our spiritual, mental and physical wellness. So, we are reminded often through ceremony that it is important to routinely take a personal inventory to make sure we do not let negativity build up. However, in today's society that is easier said than done. When I was younger I would feel really good while I was at our Stomp Grounds but a day or two later the good feelings would be gone. The stress of everyday life would leave me feeling anxious and inadequate. Historically, Cherokee people practiced positive coping skills regularly as a part of their daily living. However, as society has changed there is less emphasis on wellness and more emphasis on production so we have to create space for our own wellness.

Growing up I knew that I was not like everyone else. My clothes were hand-me-downs and I was socially awkward. I was never the funny cool guy that everyone liked. I played sports and found acceptance and comradery on the teams I played on but I often felt like I did not fit in with mainstream society. Throughout my younger years I thought that it was most important if others accepted and liked me but by relearning to Walk In Balance I have found that it only matters if I accept and like myself. I am finally free of the burdens of anxiety, resentment and fear. I am free because by following the teachings of the program I can Walk In Balance with my spirit and environment. So, let me share how I do it and hopefully it will help you too!

Gratitude

ᎠᎵᎮᎵᏍᏗ

Alihelisdi

We aspire to live in gratitude and practice it daily.

For Cherokee people, gratitude lies at the center of our culture. Cherokee people are taught that gratitude is a spiritual practice that we should focus on daily despite any adversity we are facing. From the time that we awake to our last thoughts before sleep, we are taught to appreciate all that we are blessed with. This practice has enabled us to remain positive and productive in the face of extreme hardship. Gratitude is woven into traditional Cherokee culture because we have long recognized the benefits of practicing it. Some benefits of practicing gratitude regularly that I have experienced include improved physical and psychological health. I also sleep more soundly and experience less anxiety and stress.

One example of practicing gratitude occurs at our ceremonial grounds where we are taught to spit out our first bite of food. We do this as a way to acknowledge the blessings that we have and we symbolically give some back to the earth. Of course, we are outside when we do this sitting at tables and the animals and bugs will take away the food for themselves or it will compost into the earth. Some young children will have to be reminded of the practice as everyone is hungry from playing ball and eager to eat. You will often hear the older kids remind the younger ones to spit out the first bite and let them know the reason why. This is only one of many gratitude exercises practiced while we are at ceremony. Unfortunately, we cannot be at ceremony every day and after the songs are sung and the dance is over then it is time to return to our homes and work and the chores of everyday life. However, we can continue to practice gratitude no matter where we are and that is the goal; to be grateful every day and remember all of the good things in our lives.

Unfortunately, our brains are not wired to remember the positive things in our lives so we have to be mindful of what we choose to focus on. The fact of the matter is that we always have something to be grateful for and if I am not feeling sorry for myself then I can see it. Unfortunately, we find ourselves increasingly less grateful for many reasons. One reason could be that we are targeted on a daily basis by media and ads that are designed to make us feel inadequate so that we buy whatever product is being sold. Have you ever felt like you weren't enough or that what you had wasn't enough? Well if you have then that may be by design. If everyone was just happy with what they had then many products would be left on store shelves. I have felt pressured at times to get the new thing when watching ads or looking at what others had. However, I finally realized that the new shoes or new phone or a new car would never make me feel more grateful. Instead, I needed to first appreciate the things that I already had in my life in order to feel fulfilled. Social media is another arena that can leave you feeling inadequate if you often compare your life to others.

At times I would be grateful if I was given something or if everything was going my way but what about the days when nothing goes your way? We will often find what we are looking for so even during times that we are facing adversity we can continue to see the positive things in our lives if that is what we want to see. We can live in gratitude no matter what is going on around us but we have to choose to do so. Every day when I get up I give thanks for another day on this earth and I make the decision to be grateful. Not just if everything goes my way but despite any challenges that may come I will remain grateful.

Of course, our gratitude muscle must be flexed daily and it helps to have a daily gratitude practice. Also, don't worry if you do not feel super grateful right away. Like everything it just takes practice and once your thoughts are focused on gratitude then you will soon begin to feel gratitude also. When you live in gratitude suddenly all of the minor annoyances don't bother you as much and no matter what adversity you face you know that everything will work out. This feeling and positive outlook will help you effectively manage life's ups and downs. So gratitude is really the first tool that we have to cope with an ever-changing world but we have to practice it regularly to reap the benefits. Once I started practicing gratitude regularly and really started feeling grateful then I began to receive more things in my life to be grateful for. It was as though I broke through some unseen barrier that was holding me back from accomplishing my goals and I believe it is because I was grateful for what I already had.

Another way to practice gratitude is to remind others in your life that you are grateful for them. This is very important and benefits both you and the person that you are showing gratitude toward. I am not perfect by any means but I work really hard and when someone in my life lets me know that they are appreciative of my efforts or my presence it really means a lot. It doesn't have to be a grand gesture or anything either. Just a simple "thank you, I appreciate you" will go a long way toward improving relationships with those who you value in your life. So, whether it is your parent, spouse or friend make sure you take the time to let your loved ones know that you are grateful for them as it promotes balance.

I have really worked hard to ensure that my self-worth isn't tied up in how others view me but it still feels really good to be valued. When someone lets me know that they are grateful for me then my load seems a little lighter and I approach my work with a more grateful heart. I am less annoyed to be picking up the same pile of clothes that always seems to accumulate in the corner and I am happy to get up first and make the coffee. I know that it feels risky to put yourself out there sometimes but I have never regretted saying something nice to someone. You never know how a simple gesture or kind word can turn around someone's day. I think one of the biggest mistakes that we make in relationships is assuming that others know how we feel about them. Even if they do know it is great to remind them that you are grateful to have them in your life. As I said before, our brains are not wired to remember positive things so we need to refresh our memories from time to time. Every time you take the healthy risk to let others know that you are grateful for them you are helping that other person and yourself as well. Your words are a gift and have value. Using your words regularly to uplift others will improve your own mood as well and aid you in your gratitude journey. I have heard the adage that you can't be both grateful and unhappy so I practice gratitude daily to keep my focus on my blessings. There are many different ways to practice gratitude and I have included a few that I do myself.

Action Steps

List what you are grateful for

I do a mental list every day of what I am grateful for. You can do this list verbally, mentally or you may want to write down what you are grateful for so that you remember it. In our house, we have an accomplishments/gratitude board and it helps me to remember all of the great things that occur in my life on a regular basis. One of my favorite gratitude practices is to list what I am grateful for every day when I get into the shower. Cherokee people have a very deep relationship with water and we actually have ceremonies where we go to water for healing so I feel like this is an appropriate time for a daily wellness exercise. So, while I shower and prepare for the day I just begin to list everything that I am grateful for. My list is not structured in any way and I do not pass judgment on the length or depth of my gratitude list. My gratitude list changes every day and it is very personal. Some days I might list 15 things other days 30 but the point is that I am focused on my blessings rather than anxiety or stress.

Take a gratitude picture

Pictures are a great way to memorialize what you are grateful for. This is very easy to do and it captures that moment of gratitude so that you can return to it anytime that you wish. I will also sometimes post my gratitude picture for others to enjoy.

Invite the family to practice gratitude

A great way to get your family into the gratitude mindset is to have everyone list one thing they are grateful for. This can be done before you sit down to eat or any other time that the family gathers throughout the day. This exercise takes minimal time but is a great way to interrupt the busy daily routine to refocus on gratitude. You may get some off-the-wall answers from your children like "I am glad my brother's feet don't smell today" but you may also get a valuable peek into their very busy lives. I really like this exercise because it takes literally a few minutes and it teaches the youth that gratitude is beneficial as a daily practice.

Let others know that you are grateful for them

It is important to let people in your life know that you are grateful for them and it is a very powerful gratitude practice. I know when someone tells me that they appreciate my efforts it really brightens my day. Expressing gratitude helps me to feel more optimistic because I recognize that I am not alone and it also strengthens my connections with others.

Mindfulness

ᎤᏓᏅᏘᎰᏨᎯ
Udanvtihotsvhi

We aspire to be present in this moment without judging ourselves or others.

Cherokees have always practiced mindfulness as a way to stay connected to their spirit, the creator and the environment. I was taught that it is important to be present in the moment and not be always looking too much into the future or the past. This helps me keep my stress level down because I am not always concerned with tomorrow or yesterday but instead I just focus on living this moment and this day well. It is good to put your phone away sometimes and just be quiet. Take a walk and breathe the fresh air and reconnect with your spirit without your mind obsessing over the past or things to come. Practicing mindfulness regularly has improved my life in several ways. I experience less stress and anxiety and enjoy more moments. My relationships have also improved because I am more present for myself and others. My goal is not to have small moments of mindfulness but to be able to be fully present at all times and instead have small moments where I can think ahead and be outside of myself.

In my childhood, I was encouraged to practice mindfulness while at our Stomp Grounds. I was taught to be present and experience everything without judgment. I believed that at that moment I was exactly where I was supposed to be and I was doing exactly what I was supposed to do. I remember the moments when we weren't playing ball or eating or dancing. Everything was very still except for occasional laughter around the grounds. I would sit on the ground and watch the bugs go about their work. I would often lay on the ground and watch the clouds move across the sky while the treetops swayed in the wind. It was perfect and I was content because I was free of judgment and worry.

You do not have to be at a ceremonial ground to practice mindfulness and Cherokee people have always practiced mindfulness as a part of their daily routine. I was taught that mindfulness can be practiced anywhere at any time. Whether I am weaving a basket or walking my dogs I can slow down that hamster wheel in my mind and focus on the moment. If I am walking then I can take notice of the sounds that the trees make in the wind and the leaves crunching underfoot. I take deep breaths and am often in awe of the power of nature. If I want to practice mindfulness then I do not judge the moment. I am not trying to exercise and speed walk or look at my phone to see how far I've gone or the latest post on Instagram. I just enjoy the time being me in the place that I am in and it is enough and I am enough.

Basket making and other arts are also great ways to practice mindfulness. I love the repetitive motion of weaving a basket and I can quiet my mind and just be. Sometimes I will take this time to do a gratitude exercise or positive affirmations also if I am so inclined. I do not judge my feelings whatever they are and just take the time to experience them. Like every other component of the Walking In Balance curriculum, it just takes a little practice and the decision to work on your wellness. I went through a long period where I quit practicing mindfulness regularly and began to experience anxiety and overstress. I had to finally get sick and tired of being sick and tired to make a sustainable change in my life.

My big mindfulness wake-up call came the day that I turned 30 years old. It felt like an important milestone in my life that I needed to acknowledge so I stopped and took stock of my progress. I began to look back on my adult life and was shocked when I realized that I hadn't enjoyed much of it. Don't get me wrong, I did a lot of great things and the happiest memories in my life all involved friends and family. However, during even the best moments of my life, anxiety and fear ruled the day. One of my favorite things I have ever done is to coach my children's sports teams but even during those really awesome times, I would be worried about everything. Worried about the future, worried about bills, worried whether there was enough food for the team and a thousand other things that could possibly go wrong. I was often so wrapped up in the future that I never took the time to be present for myself and my family.

Another toxic trait that I picked up over the years without realizing it is buying into the notion that being a workaholic is a good thing. As Americans, we are often taught that we are supposed to always be productive and this thinking often gets in the way of our wellness program. Whatever work or educational setting you are in make sure that you create the space to practice mindfulness. Nobody is going to set aside the time for your wellness so we have to take it upon ourselves to schedule the time. You do not need a lot of time to practice mindfulness, however. It could be as quick as a five-minute meditation in the morning or a 10-minute walk on your break or just a few minutes to take some deep breaths and re-center.

You can be mindful also without it being a structured activity. One of the things that I desperately wanted to work on was being fully present when spending time with my family. Practicing mindfulness regularly definitely helps me to be present on a more consistent basis but I also set an intention to do so. One of the biggest obstacles to overcome for me when I try to practice mindfulness is the nagging feeling that I should be doing something else. I should be working or cleaning or doing something other than what I am doing. I have to believe that the world is not going to stop turning just because I am taking 15 minutes to go for a quick walk or sit down and listen to a meditation on my phone. I also have to believe that everything happens for my highest good and I will ultimately fulfill all of my obligations right on time. However, my mind doesn't often want to accept that and I encourage myself to force things even when the timing is not right. If I allow this thinking to take hold then I try to do everything right now and just end up feeling frustrated because nothing turns out right. So, I first have to trust myself to know when to act and trust that the universe is working on my behalf.

Patience

One mindfulness tool that helps to prevent frustration is patience. Growing up I learned that there was a season for everything and things happened when they were supposed to. Our ability to practice patience can prevent us from making rash decisions out of frustration. Cherokee people have always been adept at practicing patience though I would say my generation may be less so. Our ancestors understood that the ability to accept delay without becoming frustrated or being able to tolerate provocation calmly would ultimately help us achieve our goals. Patience was also a spiritual practice because Cherokee people believed that things happened when they were supposed to regardless of our frustration. All we can do is put in the work and trust that things will work out as they should. Obsessing over timelines and things that could go wrong will only lead to frustration and unhappiness. Even though we know this it is still easy to become frustrated and the technology that we rely on now may not be helping.

There have been tremendous technological advancements made in recent years and they have been of great benefit to many but they have also changed our expectations. Whether it is food or information, we expect everything to be delivered fast and our patience seems to wear thin very quickly these days. Technological advancements have made us more dependent on instant gratification because we can have everything we want faster than ever before. This expectation of easily obtained outcomes also gives rise to frustration and risky behavior when things take more time than we are willing to spend. This is evidenced at any intersection nowadays where cars routinely continue to pass through the intersection even after the light has turned red.

I have found myself frustrated often by people, places and things because I have no control over them. I've gotten frustrated over long lines at the drive-through and when my phone or computer doesn't load fast enough. I've gotten frustrated when people do not act or respond the way that I would like. That is life. Of course, I almost always masked how I really felt but behind my smile, there was a constant stream of frustration and resentment. So I found myself frustrated very often and I grew tired of it and I set an intention to change the way that I reacted when things did not go my way. First, I began to look at my need to control. I began to delve into its origins and most importantly, how I could change it going forward. Many things that I do today are tied to my life experiences and my need to control is no different. Due to the trauma that I experienced as a child, I tried to mitigate any negativity by controlling every last detail of my life. Needless to say, this did not work and only served to make me more frustrated in the process.

So I looked back into our cultural teachings and realized that I needed to incorporate patience into my mindfulness practice. In Cherokee culture, we understand that after you do the work then things will happen when they happen and no amount of frustration or fist-shaking is going to change that. Also, by practicing patience as a lifestyle then one can avoid being routinely frustrated by our environment including the people we have to interact with daily. So how do we practice patience on a daily basis in order to avoid frustration? Have you ever been told to be patient? That is frustrating in itself if you are not taught how. So I began to look at how my ancestors were able to be patient in order to live well.

The first thing that struck me in looking at our cultural and ceremonial teachings in regarding patience is that traditional Cherokees are taught that we are only a part of the universe and not the center of it. We are no more or less important than any other creation on earth. I remember being comforted by that when I was young and I would listen to the elders speak to us (often when we were causing a ruckus). They often taught us these lessons through stories and looking back on the many teachings I received I have narrowed on three key takeaways.

First, if we trust that the universe is working on our behalf then we need not worry once our work is done. Faith is important to have so that you can let go of the need to control everything and drive yourself mad. When we plant a seed and give the seed what it needs to grow we trust that it will do so. We do not keep digging up the seed to check the progress. All we can do is our part and trust that everything else will happen as it should. So now instead of worrying if others will do their part I just focus on my work and do the best that I can and then I let it go. If I am anxious about a result then I picture in my mind the task being accomplished and I can feel a sense of gratitude as a positive result comes to fruition. This is in contrast to how I used to react which is to worry and fret and double-check and triple-check and worry some more. All this did was increase my stress and anxiety and had no bearing on the outcome at all.

Second, I learned that things will not always happen on our timeline but will happen at the time and season that is right. I mentioned learning not to overestimate my importance and accept that I have a place in this world but I am not the whole world. This teaching helps to remind me that things do not have to happen according to my timeline. Being able to accept delay without becoming frustrated takes practice but it is possible. Now, if I am stuck in a line or waiting on a result I simply focus on something else to avoid frustrating myself. If I find myself being delayed then I like to use that time to check in with myself and others. I like to take a few moments and focus on how I feel or I will connect with a friend or family member.

Third, I was taught that I have no control over anything except myself. This is another area that has frustrated me in the past but now I can practice acceptance in order to stave off those negative feelings. Acceptance of the situation can help you to avoid frustration while waiting for a result to come through. A lot of people in recovery may know this teaching also from the Serenity Prayer which states "I accept the things I cannot change." I can accept that people in my orbit may be rude, or hurtful so instead of trying to change these people I simply limit the time that I spend with them. Looking back I realize that I spent a lot of time trying to change people and things so that they are more palatable to me when I could have used my time to work on myself instead. That is really all that I have control over. Not my spouse, not my coworkers and not my friends. You can love people and give advice and guidance but ultimately we all must make our own decisions. Cherokee people have long recognized that everyone has their own journey that is sacred and it is not the Cherokee way to tell others how they should live their lives. As I said, we can provide assistance if asked but everyone's journey is personal. If I do not like what someone is doing or how they are treating me then the best thing to do is limit my time with that person instead of trying to change them. My journey has taken me many places and I have made many mistakes but I didn't change until I was ready.

Setting an Intention

Setting an intention for your day and your future is very important because life happens right? I have always felt that without an intention then it is harder to maintain a positive course because the way that our society is set up there aren't many safeguards or supportive services for people once they start heading down the wrong path. One example of this I see a lot is where youth who have no plans after school can end up drinking, developing negative coping mechanisms, running around and can end up getting into trouble. It is as though it is easier to be pulled toward negativity if you do not consciously decide to stay on a positive course. I am not saying that youth or adults who do not go to school or work or volunteer are destined for bad outcomes. However, I have seen it play out many times where those who are not actively pursuing positive growth will often find their path skewed toward negativity and risky behavior. It makes all the difference what our intentions are and if we are living our life with a purpose.

Cherokee people have always believed that it is important to start your day in a good way by giving thanks and setting an intention for how you want to feel and what you want to accomplish. When I was young I was taught that if I do not decide what I want for myself then others would decide for me. Over time, however, I started thinking that life just happened to me instead of believing that I was in control of my destiny. This of course is not true and each of us gets to decide how we want to feel and who we want to be and what we will accomplish. Yes, there are barriers and it will take work but we will succeed if we intend to. It is all about what we choose to focus on and if we are looking for barriers then that is what we will find, conversely, if we are looking for solutions then we will find those as well.

By setting an intention for what you want in life you are deciding right there at that moment how your life will go. Not just if everything is easy and goes your way but when we set our intention we are declaring that no matter what; this is who and what I am going to be. For instance, this morning I set an intention to practice self-compassion, be present for myself and my family and enjoy my day. I didn't think about or qualify that statement by adding "as long as everyone is nice to me and there is no traffic and nobody upsets me and I accomplish everything on my to-do list." No. I am saying that no matter what I am going to enjoy this day. This is important because life's unexpected challenges can and will arise but I have already set my intention so I am going to practice self-compassion, be present and enjoy my day as I deal with flat tires and missed deadlines and rude people and anything else that life can throw at me. Without this intention for my day and my future then I am really at the mercy of the wind as I can be blown in any direction and who knows how I will feel or what I will accomplish.

It is also important for me to be mindful when I am setting my intentions in order to stay in line with my spiritual purpose. I will cover this more later when I talk about spiritual wellness but I do not set intentions that go against my values or take me off of my spiritual path. I set intentions to accomplish my goals and be of service. I set intentions to be present for my family and practice gratitude. I set intentions to live and Walk In Balance so that I can live a fulfilled life of wellness. I sincerely believe that if I remain close to my spirit and live in balance and gratitude then the universe will meet me halfway. I set intentions to realize goals that I set in the pursuit of my passions at home and also in educational and work settings. The distinction between this and just setting intentions to get money is that as long as I am continuing to grow and Walk In Balance then I will always have everything that I need. So my intentions set my focus and energy toward what I will pursue that day. With my other intentions for this day, I also set an intention to write and practice self-care and here I am writing. This is a big deal. After all, my intentions make me feel powerful because I get to decide what I will do. Others can ask for my time but I can and do say "no" if I have something scheduled or have an intention set for that time. Saying "no" takes practice also if you are a people pleaser like me but it does get easier.

So, every day make that decision and set an intention for what you want for yourself. You can do this when you are enjoying your morning coffee, during meditation or prayer or while you drive to work. If we can take moments where we are quiet and still then it is easier for us to stay in touch with our spirit and our emotions. I really enjoy the time that I have to myself to do these exercises where in the past the stillness and silence were really uncomfortable because I was not comfortable with myself. Love yourself and show yourself compassion. Listen to your spirit and do not shut down your emotions. When we practice mindfulness we can really be in tune with our spirit and can set intentions that will guide our days and ensure that we are successful in all of our endeavors.

Action Steps

It is hard to be able to find balance, connect with your spirit and be at peace when your thoughts are racing and distracting you from your purpose. This has happened to me a lot over the years and I would often get down on myself for not having better mental discipline but I have found several ways to practice mindfulness, lower my stress level and reduce anxiety.

Mindfulness Meditation

One of my favorite things to do is take a 5 or 10-minute mindfulness break throughout the day to meditate and re-center. In a perfect world we could find time to meditate three times a day for a few minutes but even meditating once a day will help reduce anxiety and help us remember our purpose. Meditating in the morning helps me to set an intention for the day and be aware of my body and feelings and gives me direction. When I meditate at noon I find that I can bring into focus my morning and re-center if needed. If I have had a troubled morning then I can avoid carrying that moment into the rest of my day. If I have had a good morning then meditation helps me to stay in that moment and feeling. When I meditate at night I get an opportunity to shake off and release any feelings of anxiousness and bring myself into balance with my spirit before I sleep. This helps me to enjoy a peaceful and restful sleep.

So, no matter when you meditate there are opportunities to be present throughout the day and enjoy your lives. When I meditate, I sit or lie still with my eyes closed and I will either play some positive affirmations or soft music and just focus on my breathing. Since I am very busy and I move and think fast I have noticed that my breaths are often quick and shallow. So, by taking the time to slow my breathing down and slow my mind down I am able to be present. I take 5 or 10 minutes and breathe deeply while enjoying any sensations that my body is feeling. I do not judge my thoughts during this time and if my mind begins to race I simply refocus on the present. In the beginning, I really benefitted from guided meditations but no matter how you meditate just slowing your breathing and your thoughts down will definitely help you to relax and be present.

Mindfulness Crafting

I have been doing this mindfulness exercise since I was young and I really feel different when I am crafting. My favorite mindfulness craft is basket making and I love how the repetitive motion of weaving a basket helps me to slow my mind and my breathing down and just focus on being present. I was taught when I was young that when we make or create something we should think positively because we transfer that energy into our craft. So whether I am cooking, braiding my hair or making a basket I practice mindfulness without judgment and allow good energy to flow through me. Being creative is a great way to cope positively if you are facing adversity.

Take a Mindfulness Walk

Walking is one of the best ways that I have found to help me maintain a connection to my spirit and the universe. When I take a mindfulness walk I do not check my phone or look to see how many steps I've taken. I just let myself be in nature and take notice of my surroundings and after a while, I can feel my stress and anxiety begin to subside. I just give my mind a break and after my walk, I feel better and my mind is clearer. If I have something heavy on my mind a mindfulness walk often helps me to see things better.

Practice Patience

Practicing patience helps me to keep my thoughts focused on what I am doing instead of what others are doing and things that may or may not happen. I do my work and then trust that the universe will meet me halfway. Also, I work on trusting my own intuition that I will know when it is time to act so I do not have to constantly worry. I accept my present situation and also accept that things may not happen when I want but will happen when the time is right. If I feel myself getting impatient then I repeat the mantra “slow is smooth and smooth is fast” to remind myself that I do not need to be in a hurry and I am okay.

Self-Compassion

ᎠᏩᏓᏙᎵᏣᏗ
Awadadolitsati

We aspire to be compassionate to ourselves at all times. We aspire to forgive, accept and love ourselves unconditionally.

I came to learn about self-compassion through traditional teachings that stressed the importance of treating ourselves in a good way. This is a skill that can be learned, however, it must also be practiced to produce any measurable benefit. Though I wanted to be nice to myself and say nice things to myself, somewhere along the way I began to be overly critical, judgmental and less patient with myself. This negative self-talk that was the result of trauma and other societal factors did not serve me and kept me feeling inadequate and depressed. At the time I thought that I was motivating myself to be better and do better but looking back now I can see that I was only hurting myself and making my goals much harder to attain. You see, while I had lofty goals I also had unreasonable expectations for achieving them which kept me feeling inferior and unworthy. Then, while I became mired in this self-defeating cycle I would be overly critical and judgmental because I was not achieving what I had set out to do. All of this combined to do quite a number on my self-esteem and took a bit of time to heal from.

I have always tried to be a good friend and family member. If someone in my life was hurting or needed encouragement I was right there with a kind word and understanding. Unfortunately, I was not always as compassionate with myself which is a lonely place to be especially if you do not have people in your life who build you up. Honestly, though, it is nobody's job to make sure that I am happy and it is up to us to take responsibility for our own happiness. We have to be our own cheerleaders and be able to comfort ourselves and pick ourselves up when times are tough which seems to happen often these days.

Now I make sure to show compassion to myself every day and treat myself as I would a family member or best friend. So for me, this looks like instead of saying, "man that was stupid now I messed up everything," I instead say, "well that didn't go according to plan but I learned a lot and I am proud of myself for trying." I really am proud of myself, every day. I am proud to be a friend to myself because it has totally changed my outlook on life. I have been in great positions before that many would envy but it felt like my own personal hell because my perception was skewed by negative self-talk and criticism. This kept me from enjoying anything, especially my accomplishments because I could only think of why I didn't do it sooner. So instead of motivating me, my self-criticism only held me back and made me feel bad about myself. I am now a huge proponent of self-compassion and it is my hope that everyone gets to experience the joy of having yourself as a best friend. I accomplish this through several ways, including positive self-talk, self-acceptance, confidence and forgiveness. Some of the many benefits that I have experienced from regularly practicing self-compassion are increased self-confidence, improved body image and I am also more resilient.

Self-Acceptance

I am happy to be able to say that I accept and love myself. It is amazing to say that really because for most of my life that wasn't the case. As far back as I can remember I never liked myself and often wished that I was someone else. I never liked the way that I looked or my personality or my circumstances. I developed this feeling early in life but I cannot say exactly when or why. I do remember feeling this way at an early age when I was placed in an Indian boarding school with my siblings. My roommate and I were subjected to abuse on a routine basis and I remember back then feeling as if there was something wrong with me and wishing that I was someone else. This feeling persisted for much of my life though I would often mask it because I couldn't figure out how to fix it. It is sad that I felt that way and that others feel this way about themselves but I am happy to say that we can change it. That's the headline.

It wasn't supposed to be this way. I always meant to love and accept myself and I was going to do it as soon as I was in shape, and I had the perfect job and the perfect spouse and a lot of money. However, no matter what I accomplished it was never good enough because I was fundamentally flawed. Rather, it was my thinking that was flawed and if I held onto those same beliefs about myself then I would probably be dead by now. It is a dangerous thing to not accept yourself and always wish to be something different because you are making your choices from a plane where success is very unlikely. So, instead of changing my face and my hair and my personality and my voice and the way I laughed and my smile, I decided to change my thinking and self-talk.

The first time that I was told to say something nice about myself was when I was a teenager and I was in rehab in Oakland, California. I had already figured out how to self-medicate and needless to say that landed me in several institutions throughout my life. This particular rehab was for teenagers and the staff told me that every time I passed under a doorway I had to say something nice about myself. I remember the first time I had to do it I just stood there for several minutes unable to come up with one thing that I liked about myself. I don't remember what I eventually muttered to get them off my back but I do remember alarm bells going off inside my head because even though I considered myself intelligent I couldn't even fake it. This went on for most of my life to varying degrees and I look back now and wish that I would have been kinder to myself but having gone through that now helps me help others.

I think the saddest thing would be if I had gone my whole life and not liked the person that I was. However, I am happy to report that such is not the case and I accept and love the person I am and the person that I was then. I accept and love my body at my current weight and if I am heavier or lighter. I accept my physical appearance even though one eye is wonky and seems to have a life of its own sometimes. I accept that I am socially awkward and never know the clever thing to say, until much later that is. I accept my body doesn't move as fast as it once did but has helped me survive despite my repeated attempts to self-destruct. I accept and love my smile whereas before I hated the sight of it. So, in short, I am free of the bondages of self-criticism and self-loathing. Yes, I have bad moments but I rarely have a bad day and never a bad week. I get to choose how I feel now because I practice self-acceptance daily.

Acceptance does not mean we are resigned to any situation and just because we love and accept our body does not mean that we do not work to achieve physical fitness. I believe it is natural to want to improve certain things but it is important to love and accept ourselves along the way. So for me this means appreciating and accepting the changes that my body goes through, though, it does take some practice. I remember when I first started to get gray hair in my early thirties and I started dying it because I couldn't accept that I was getting older. I think part of it was regret about my misspent youth and part of it was vanity. Either way, it was ridiculous because I would spend a lot of time and energy worrying about it instead of accepting and embracing the changes that my body is going through. I am not against dying hair and I even rocked some blue hair back in the '90s. For me, it was more about the inability to accept and love myself for how I was.

I realize now that if my self-worth is only derived from how I look then it is all downhill from here. I realized that I was getting older when I began to look for a place to sit to tie my shoe and I started to grunt when I got up. Also, my joints often sound like rice crispies and it seems to get harder and harder to lose weight. Such is life and I want to enjoy it and accept my body no matter what. Now, my value as a human being is not derived from how I look or how much money I have, or my job. My worth comes from who I am as a person and whether or not I love, accept and respect that person.

So my self-acceptance journey started with an intention to love and accept myself because I was tired of being so self-critical. What a waste of energy. Once I set my intention I had to begin practicing it which meant a lot of meditation and positive affirmations. I needed a way to remember to say positive affirmations to myself so I decided to say them every time I washed my hands. I mentioned before that Cherokee people have a very deep relationship with water and there are healing ceremonies that involve going to water so I thought that it was an appropriate time. I started with affirmations directed at my appearance, personality and my anxiety as these 3 areas of my life brought me no joy at all and I wanted to change that. Have you ever walked into a bathroom and seen a guy talking to himself? Well, that guy might have been me though I quickly learned that it was easier to say my affirmations in my head.

I began with simple affirmations such as "I am handsome" and "I love and accept my body." Also, I would say "I love my smile and like showing it to the world." Then for my anxiety I would say "I am safe" and "I can handle any challenge that comes my way" or "everything works out for my highest good." These are just a few examples as

I would usually say about 10 affirmations while taking a breath in between and there were many variations of each. The point is that I verbalized how I wanted to feel about myself and my abilities and began to speak it into existence. Of course, in the beginning, I did not believe any of it but I was determined to change how I felt about myself. So this went on for maybe a month saying affirmations every time I washed my hands and then I noticed a change. The first thing I noticed was that I started to believe what I was saying because it no longer felt ridiculous or like I was lying. Next, I noticed that my self-confidence and self-acceptance began to improve as I really began to feel handsome and capable. I am not delusional and have not applied to any modeling agencies but I am happy with the way that I look and talk and smile for the first time in my life and that is a huge deal. My symptoms of anxiety have also improved as I realized that it had no control over me and I was capable of navigating all of life's challenges successfully.

Self-Talk

You know that voice that you have inside your head? The one that communicates the thousands of thoughts that we have daily? Aside from communicating mundane things like "I feel like pizza for lunch" or "now I feel like something sweet" (yes I think about food a lot). That voice could be contributing to your feelings of inadequacy if it sounds like "ugh I am fat, I hate my body" or "why do bad things always happen to me?" How you talk to yourself could very well determine what kind of life you have and whether or not you enjoy it. Cherokee people have long understood that our words and thoughts have power and it will greatly benefit us if we can make sure they are positive.

We have thousands of thoughts that run through our heads daily and if those thoughts are mostly negative then that could have an impact on your mental, emotional and physical health. How we talk to ourselves matters because our thoughts become intentions and actions. If we think negatively then our body will respond accordingly to those negative thoughts and if our body is constantly on edge then that could affect our physical health. I can make things harder or more manageable depending on how I approach them and talk to myself about them. If I spill my coffee I can start cussing in my head and immediately stress myself out or I can say "ope, oh well let me clean that up no big deal." This may seem like a little thing with no long-term consequences but when you think about all of the moments that you have throughout the day and if you talk to yourself negatively about a majority of them then you are living in a constant state of stress. This can negatively affect your mental, emotional and physical health.

So how do we go about changing our self-talk to a more positive and compassionate voice? First, I believe it helps to set an intention. For myself, I wanted my self-talk to reflect my values and be compassionate. So my intention was "I will speak to myself in a positive way and I will show compassion to myself." Setting an intention made it clear to me what my goal was so that I had a way to keep myself accountable and heading in the right direction. Next, I began to highlight anytime that my self-talk was negative or self-defeating. One thing that I was able to identify right away was when I would think "great it is gonna be one of those days." I would say this to myself over the most minor occurrences like spilled coffee or a flat tire. This self-talk really affected me because instead of shaking off whatever small inconvenience I was experiencing I would instead give it power and let it ruin my day.

Now, my self-talk is overwhelmingly positive due to the work that I have put in to change it. I still have an initial negative reaction sometimes but within a few moments, I can recognize my negative self-talk, evaluate it and change it to positive self-talk. This process has changed my life for the better. I am more comfortable taking healthy risks. I am more confident in my appearance and skillset and I feel happier and more grateful. Sounds like a lot of progress due to one simple change right? There are many benefits of positive self-talk and I wish that I worked on this earlier in my life. See what I did there? That statement is rooted in regret and though it may not seem like a big deal it diminishes the progress that I have made because of the negative connotation associated with wishing that I had made these changes earlier. So, I would follow up my thought about wishing I had worked on this earlier with "but I am just happy that I use more positive self-talk now." There, I fixed it. So, instead of my last thought on the subject being negative because I did not make these changes earlier I instead focus on the progress I am making now. It's all about focus. If we focus on our progress instead of our mistakes we give ourselves the strength and energy to keep moving in a positive direction.

So how do we accomplish this? For me, it started with being able to identify whether my self-talk was positive or negative. So, I began to be more mindful of my thoughts and started to take notice of when my self-talk was negative. I also noticed how it made me feel. However, one of the biggest wow moments came when I was hooked up to monitors because I was about to undergo a medical procedure. I wasn't really nervous but for some reason an old memory where I said something that I thought was dumb crossed my mind and I could still feel the embarrassment all these years later. Ordinarily, I might not have taken note of this thought had I not been all wired up, literally, but I noticed a change on the monitor when these negative thoughts came up. My heart rate and blood pressure increased where everything was stable earlier. This happened a few times before my procedure was over and really made me realize the toll that negative thinking takes on my body. I realized that over time I could see an increased probability of physical health problems associated with my negative thinking.

I then began to write down my negative thoughts. This helped me be able to recognize them in the future. I am a visual person so it helps me to see something in writing in order to remember it. After a while, I started to recognize when I had negative and anxious thoughts and I could look at those thoughts real quick and change them if need be. For instance, I am not a big fan of heights and there is a big mountain range between Thermal, California where I worked and Temecula, California where we would often go to coach various sports. You could of course drive around the mountains or go through the pass which involved traveling up switchbacks overlooking the valley which is a beautiful view for those who are not deathly afraid of heights. I always chose to drive around the mountains but many of those I traveled with opted instead to go over the mountain because "you could save ten minutes." Are you serious? I often thought to myself. Who cares about 10 minutes when you have to go up and over a huge mountain? I remember thinking. Well, it turns out a lot of people because we went over that mountain a lot. In the beginning, my mind would often flash to worst-case scenarios which usually included visuals of our SUV rolling over the side of one of the huge drop-offs. I hated how the whole process made me feel so I decided to do something about it.

I could either refuse to drive or ride with people going over the mountain, go over the mountain riddled with anxiety while resenting my coworkers, or change my thinking. I chose the latter and that choice still echoes in my life today. I started to change my thinking by writing down my negative and anxious thoughts along with positive alternatives. For instance, when I would have an anxious thought about the trip I would instead say to myself "I am safe. I have made this trip many times with no problem and this will be no different." I would also envision myself driving successfully over the pass while admiring the beautiful views and feel the gratitude for having accomplished something that was challenging. That is indeed what it was; a challenge. So that is how I approached it instead of looking at it like a problem.

So away we went. Up the steep hill until we hit the switchbacks and I veered right following the edge of the mountain but instead of looking over the edge I focused on the road in front of me and reminded myself that "I am safe. I am a good driver. I have made this trip many times. This is no big deal. I am enjoying myself." This went on for several minutes as we went back and forth winding up the mountain and then we were at the top. Yes, my hands were sweaty but we were safe and I was proud of myself and I told myself so. I have since made this trip many more times and it has gotten easier every time. So instead of letting my thoughts make me anxious and then resenting my coworkers for deciding on that route and then getting mad at myself for my anxious thoughts and feelings, I decided to talk to myself more positively. I still practice positive self-talk and I am a much happier and more accomplished person because of it. So remember, if we talk to ourselves negatively then we will get negative results but if we practice positive self-talk then there is no limit to what we can accomplish.

Self-Confidence

I became more self-confident by practicing self-compassion. In my youth, I thought that it was perhaps something you were born with. A gene that was passed down from your confident parents. I seemed to only inherit anxiety but when I was around confident people I was pleased to see someone sure of themselves and I wanted what they had. They believed in themselves and practiced self-acceptance. Many people buy into the adage "fake it until you make it" so I decided to give it a try. Outwardly, I tried to portray someone confident but I am sure people could see through the façade as I often came off as braggadocious instead. This went on for some time and I had all but given up trying to build self-confidence when I came upon it by happenstance.

It is when I began to practice self-compassion in earnest that my self-confidence began to rise. In the past, I had levels of self-confidence in different areas but overall I would not have described myself as confident. My communication skills were also subpar which made me hesitant to share in different situations. This also served to keep me isolated from others. However, all of that changed when I began to practice self-compassion and self-acceptance. Learning to accept my limitations while playing to my strengths helped me to find my voice. Practicing self-compassion daily has given me the motivation to build upon my successes and take healthy risks. It helps to know who you are and what you stand for. A non-judgmental honest assessment of your strengths and limitations will enable you to set attainable goals so that you do not set yourself up for failure. Once I began to accept who I was and be compassionate to myself I no longer felt the need to compare myself to others. This helped my self-confidence a great deal. I no longer felt like I was in a race. I was on an awesome journey and I determined where it would lead. Previously, I felt like I had to compete with others but after learning to accept myself I began to realize that each of our journeys are sacred and personal.

Another benefit of my improved self-confidence is that I have been able to overcome several of my limiting beliefs. Throughout my life, I developed limiting self-beliefs that were meant to protect me but ended up limiting my potential instead. For instance, I experienced loss in my childhood so I made sure I never got too close to anyone so that I wouldn't get hurt again. I experienced trauma in my early years that left me with a fear of failure so I didn't take many healthy risks and missed out on several opportunities. I also developed other limiting beliefs in adulthood that stymied my progress. One of them was that I don't have the time to work on my physical fitness. Another is that technical pursuits are outside the realm of possibility for me. With my newfound self-confidence, I am able to overcome all of these limiting beliefs and achieve my goals.

I now have close relationships with friends and family without fear of rejection or hurt. I no longer let my fear of failure prevent me from taking a healthy risk as I welcome the opportunity to step up to the challenge and work through adversity. I also make time for my physical health and I always find technical pursuits are easier than I made them out to be. So, I encourage you to identify any limiting beliefs that you may have so that you can judge whether that belief is helping you reach your goals or holding you back. Once you identify these false beliefs about yourself you can use your tools to create new beliefs about yourself. Positive affirmations really helped me in this area as I began to speak into existence my new beliefs about myself. Some of these include "I am confident," I am worthy of love" and "I no longer crave health-destroying junk food" just to name a few. However, you can tailor this exercise to what you want to work on and what new beliefs you want to create about yourself and your environment.

Forgiveness

It isn't just anxiety about the future that can rob me of my joy, however. Often it seemed as though anytime that I wasn't worried about the future then I was focusing too much on the past. Regret and resentment were often on my mind. Of course, being a recovering alcoholic means that I do have much to regret but I also know that if I focus too much on my regrets and resentments then that will cloud my future.

When Cherokee people attend ceremony at our Stomp Grounds we are encouraged to forgive ourselves and others so that we are not bound to those negative events. However, resentment is a hell of a drug. I don't know why but I would hold onto it and covet it like it was sacred. Even after I learned that I could forgive I would often hold onto resentment because the toxicity somehow made me feel better. Like I had some power. Of course, I know now that I was only destroying myself from the inside out and I was letting those who hurt me win again. So, I finally got to the point where I was sick and tired of being sick and tired. My friend John Aaron used to tell me that when it hurts enough then you will make a change. Well, all of the resentment that I carried around hurt like heck and it nearly killed me.

So, I finally decided to quit punishing myself and decided to forgive. The act of forgiveness was not to let those who wronged me off the hook but instead free myself from the bondage of pain and toxicity. Cherokee people have long recognized how regret and resentment can prevent us from living in balance and that is why forgiveness is practiced at our ceremonial grounds. We are taught to let go of regret and resentment when we practice our ceremonial ways because they can disrupt our spiritual connection. Someone who is not familiar with our ceremonial practices may look from the outside and see us eating and playing ball and dancing but that is only part of the process. While we do those things we are taught to forgive others and practice empathy, humility and kindness. I know that it can be hard to forgive others but I finally grew tired of letting others live rent-free in my head. So, what helps me now is to ask myself if being angry or resentful is helping me to reach my goals. My goal is to live a fulfilled life of wellness so the answer is always no. Once I can frame the issue in a way that enables me to focus on the benefits of forgiveness then the process is easier. Forgiving others continues to be an ongoing process and it has taken a lot of practice but what about forgiving myself for past mistakes?

Another part of practicing self-compassion is allowing ourselves to grow and learn and making mistakes is often a part of that process. Some of us may not have been taught how to Walk In Balance and may have hurt ourselves and others because we coped in negative ways. Simply put "we didn't know what we didn't know." Of course, in our youth, many of us feel like we have it all figured out but when we can finally accept that we know only a little and will continue to learn forever, then we are on the right path. So, while clumsily fumbling around the world we often make mistakes. However, learning from your mistakes and setting an intention to do better puts us on the road to enlightenment. One barrier to that is regret and shame for the mistakes that we have made. However, carrying that burden only serves to slow our progress and gets in the way of our wellness and service to others. So, at some point, each person must decide when they have endured enough torment and unshoulder that burden. So when do you know if you have suffered and blamed yourself enough that you can start to forgive yourself? I would say immediately and often. Shame and guilt serve no purpose and if it is your intention to learn and do no harm then you deserve to walk without that negativity weighing you down. So, whether it is nightly, weekly or monthly, make sure you are taking time to forgive yourself and others as we continue to heal and progress.

Action Steps

List what went well today

We all try so hard and rarely take the time to appreciate our efforts. I like to take stock at the end of the day and congratulate myself on a job well done because I did my best. This helps me to refocus my anxious thoughts about the future to instead appreciate everything that went well on this day. It also helps me end the day feeling accomplished and I appreciate everything that did go well instead of what I did not get done. This helps me relax and I enjoy a more restful sleep.

Practice forgiveness

Regret and resentment are barriers to wellness. Forgiving yourself and others will help you to reach your wellness goals faster as you transition from negativity to a more positive existence. Releasing yourself from the bondage of resentment and anger will enable you to live a life with lower stress and anxiety. It also promotes positive thinking. There are many ways to practice forgiveness. One of the ways that I practice forgiveness is by practicing empathy as that helps me to see things from other's perspectives and helps me to realize that we are all flawed and make mistakes. This doesn't mean I have to be best friends with those who have wronged me but I can at least understand that they may be in pain also. Next, I focus on forgiveness when meditating and praying while at ceremony or while I am practicing spiritual wellness. I try to forgive every few days. I forgive everyone. I forgive myself if I made a mistake. I forgive my spouse if she unintentionally hurt my feelings. I forgive the person who honked at me in the car line this morning because I realize now that harboring resentment only hurts me.

Practice Self-acceptance

Give yourself permission to be human. Though it may look like it on social media, none of us are perfect. It is helpful if you can resist comparing yourself to others as it will only serve to make you feel bad about yourself. Instead, I focus on myself and practice self-acceptance daily. Be kind to yourself and practice positive self-talk. Tell yourself you are worthy and beautiful. Practicing self-compassion will help you to accept and love the person that you are.

View Challenges as opportunities

Our lives are really about focus. What we focus on and how we talk to ourselves about our lives determines whether we live in peace or stress. I used to say "everything would be great if that didn't happen" or if "they didn't make me mad." Life happens but it is how we react to it that determines our happiness. Now, I view adversity as a challenge instead of a problem and it is an opportunity to learn and increase my skill set. By framing these challenges in a more positive light I approach my work with more energy and a more compassionate voice.

Practice positive affirmations

This continues to be one of the most rewarding exercises that I do to improve my self-talk, self-confidence and self-compassion. I began by practicing positive affirmations every time I wash my hands. Now, I do them throughout the day whenever I want to focus on the positive. The awesome thing about positive affirmations is that you can tailor them to any situation that you want to improve. Just start searching "positive affirmations" on the internet and you will get a wide range of examples. You can also search positive affirmations for specific areas such as self-acceptance, anxiety or gratitude. Write down 5 or 10 that you want to repeat to yourself every day. When I first began to practice positive affirmations I did not necessarily believe them but after about a month I started to believe them and my self-acceptance and self-confidence increased.

Wellness

ᏙᎯ ᏃᏛᏏᏕᎬᎢ
Tohi nodvhnadegvi

We aspire to be spiritually, mentally, physically, emotionally and socially well.

Traditionally, there was an emphasis placed on wellness as that was our lifelong ambition. Not wealth or notoriety or power. It was the ability to be well, feel well and live in balance that was the intention and purpose of our culture. As I mentioned before, Cherokee culture and ceremonial practices help us to live a fulfilled life of wellness. However, it is not any one area of wellness that produces the desired outcome but the balance of our physical, emotional, mental, spiritual and social wellness. I know this seems like a lot to worry about but it is pretty simple to incorporate into your day.

Spiritual Wellness

In my youth, I thought of spiritual wellness as just my relationship with the Creator. However, spiritual wellness also encompasses our relationship with our own spirit as we work toward identifying and fulfilling our spiritual purpose. So, if we are spiritually well then we are aligned with our higher power, to our own spirit and to others as well. My experiences at many ceremonies over the years helped me to connect with my spirit and but I lost the connection when I began to use alcohol. In sobriety, I have once again found my spiritual connection and through prayer and meditation, I was able to identify my spiritual purpose.

The term spiritually well was never used when I was young. We participated in ceremonies because it was our way and that was it. Wellness and balance are so engrained in Cherokee culture and spirituality that it isn't even really mentioned. You just know. This is just the way that we do these things as a way to stay connected. However, the reason that I am writing down these teachings now is that our lives have changed so drastically that we cannot take for granted that everyone automatically understands why we practice our ceremonies and what they mean. Also, as society continues to evolve many cultural teachings are not perpetuated outside of ceremony. So, in your everyday life, you may not have any exposure to these teachings. Without articulating these teachings it would take years of living traditionally to fully understand how we maintain our spiritual connection. So many stories and songs and much prayer and meditation make up the essence of our spirituality. So I think it is important to communicate these teachings so that everyone can understand why spiritual connection is important and how to achieve it.

For me, spiritual wellness involves my connection with the creator, my connection with my own spirit and identifying and fulfilling my spiritual purpose. The first part I won't go into too much detail about because I believe everyone's connection with their higher power is deeply personal. Suffice it to say that I attend ceremony in order to stay connected to the creator but I find spiritual connection also when the sun hits my face, when the trees speak overhead and you can hear leaves rustling and also when I go to water. I was able to connect with my own spirit when I was young and would attend traditional ceremonies. I felt at one with my spirit and I felt that it was my spiritual calling to help others. However, instead of following my spiritual calling, I would often go with the crowd in order to be accepted by my peers. I thought that was more important to be tough even though I did not like to fight anyone. Eventually, living to please others separated me from my spirit and I lost that connection for a while.

I am happy to say now that I am once again connected to my spirit and am fulfilling what I believe to be my spiritual purpose. I believe it is my purpose in life to help others in any way that I can and that often means sharing the Walking In Balance teachings with others so that they may live a fulfilled life of wellness.

Emotional Wellness

Traditionally, Cherokee healers would consider many things when deciding how to aid someone who was ill including emotional wellness. Current medical care often constitutes treating the symptoms of whatever is ailing you. Historically, however, traditional healers took more time to address the entire well-being of those in their care. This meant asking about many things including relationships, thoughts, feelings and emotions. Emotional wellness is an integral component of the wellness spectrum and I feel as though it is often the most overlooked. Emotional wellness is a broad topic that includes one's ability to recognize, accept and express their emotions and feelings. In hindsight, I can trace many problems that occurred in my life back to the fact that I was emotionally unwell. So when did everything go off track? I believe that the trauma that I endured as a youth led me to develop survival skills that included suppressing my emotions because they were very complicated and

I did not have the skills to process them. I was so overwhelmed that if I let myself feel anything at all then I might just explode.

I kept my defensive walls up for most of my life. I developed this defense mechanism early on and it helped me to cope with situations that were beyond my pay grade. I cannot blame myself for developing these survival skills, however, because they did help me to survive. After a while, though, these defense mechanisms began to do more harm than good. I had built such strong defensive walls around myself that I could not break them down. This meant that many thoughts, feelings and emotions were suppressed and not expressed in a healthy way. Over time I would require help to keep my emotions at bay and that meant alcohol and drugs. I floated through life completely disconnected from my emotions and feelings which kept me isolated from everyone else in my life as well. This is a lonely way to live and it would have been a tragedy had I gone on like that forever. Unfortunately, many among us also remain disconnected from themselves and others because they know no other way. But there is another way and it saved my life.

For me, the first step involved getting to know myself again including my feelings and emotions. This process took time and patience because I was so used to suppressing everything. The only emotions I was familiar with were anger and fear though there were times in between when I experienced enjoyment. This left a vast amount of emotions and feelings that went unrecognized or acknowledged because everything turned into anger as that was most comfortable. Anger made me feel like I had some power but the reality is that my anger was controlling me. So, recognizing when I was experiencing sadness or grief or excitement or jealousy was important because I couldn't improve my emotional health if I couldn't name my emotions and feelings. Once I was able to acknowledge my emotions and feelings I began the work of letting myself experience them. This took practice because I have patterns of behavior and defense mechanisms that would kick in when things became uncomfortable. Some of these included keeping everyone at a distance so that I wouldn't have to experience any uncomfortable feelings and also shutting down and quitting. Quitting had long been a way for me to escape any situation where I felt uncomfortable which meant I quit a lot. Many of us develop negative coping skills and defense mechanisms but we can replace them with healthy ways to cope. For me, this meant talking.

I have never been one to talk about my emotions or feelings as I was trying to protect myself and also societal norms dictate that men weren't supposed to do that. Yelling and punching holes in walls were acceptable ways to communicate but talking about your feelings was not. This wasn't always the case, though, because Cherokee people have always recognized the importance of talk therapy. Whether you talk to a family member, an elder or a healer all that matters is that you acknowledge your feelings and express them. Communicating feelings and emotions has fallen out of style in today's society however as we have become reliant on quick fixes and self-medicating. Sadly many people are too busy trying to keep a roof over their heads that they often feel like they don't have time for feelings and emotions and communication. However, I know that my health and wellness depend on real communication so if I do not have the time to communicate in a real way how I am feeling then I have to make time. When I communicate in a real way what I am feeling then I am connecting with others and validating the part of myself that was shut down for so long.

What this process has done for me is it has allowed me to validate and process my feelings and emotions. Once I know why I am feeling a certain way then I can work on the root causes if need be. For instance, where before I would feel shameful when I became jealous and shut everything down I now let myself experience jealousy. I get to look at it in a non-judgmental way and examine why am feeling the way that I am. Jealousy is a natural reaction and we shouldn't judge ourselves for our feelings. Am I jealous because they are something that I am not? If I desire the skills that others have then I need to put in the work to get where they are. If I am jealous because someone has a thing that I desire then I get to work on my gratitude for what I already have. The important thing is that I acknowledge my feelings and I get to work on them so that I improve myself and am not overwhelmed.

Without acknowledging and accepting my feelings then I am allowing negative patterns to continue because the root cause isn't being addressed. For instance, staying on the topic of jealousy I remember attending a training some years back on the Rincon Indian Reservation. The presenter was a Caucasian man and the first thing he said was "Indians are like crabs in a bucket because every time an Indian tries to rise up another Indian will always reach up to pull them down." I remember that I was really offended at the time. Who does this guy think he is? I thought to myself. After a few minutes of being angry, I decided to look inward and think about what he said. I did not feel like it was accurate or fair to characterize all Native people in this way but I realized that if I really felt that way then I should look at myself and see. So, I thought about it and began to examine whether I behaved in this way. When someone posts things on Facebook am I happy for them? Am I supportive or judgmental? After some self-reflection, I determined that I was supportive overall but there were times when I had jealous feelings and so I decided to examine that.

I do not want to be a crab in the bucket so if I want different results then I have to do the work.

Now, because I work with my emotions and feelings instead of suppressing them I no longer am afraid of them and I am much happier for it. Now I let my emotions help me to identify areas where I get to continue working on myself instead of just being ashamed and judging others. I can live in balance and when I am balanced then I am supportive and non-judgmental of those around me. When I am emotionally well then my thoughts and actions are filled with compassion and empathy instead of judgment and I no longer have to be ashamed of how I feel.

At the beginning of my lunch break, I take just a few minutes and close my eyes and take some deep breaths. After I take a few minutes to quiet my mind and calm my body I will often take a quick inventory of my morning. How do I feel? Do I feel balanced? Maybe someone or something made me angry or I am annoyed. Whatever I am feeling I accept it and if I need assistance processing my feelings then I can speak to someone I trust. Now, anger and irritation do not control my life because I can see that these feelings are just trying to tell me something. For instance, just yesterday I had a visit with a family member who was ill and I then came home not aware of any outstanding feelings or emotions of note. However, a little later in the day, I found myself annoyed and impatient and my spouse helped me realize that I was actually sad from my visit earlier. I was annoyed because some feelings are uncomfortable but once I realized it I was able to process my feelings, then practice self-compassion and self-care and enjoy the rest of my day. I no longer make a habit of ignoring my feelings and emotions because I recognize that my mind, body and spirit are trying to tell me something important.

Mental Wellness

Cherokee people have been able to cope with the stresses that accompanied many years of adversity because we have long recognized the importance of being mentally well. Despite this adversity, we were able to remain productive and contribute positively because of the protective factors that our cultural teachings provided. However, as these teachings fell out of favor for dominant societal teachings many came to view traditional ways as unnecessary. Thankfully, there are many things that you can do to improve your mental wellness anytime that you want. The goal is to successfully manage our lives despite any illness or adversity that we may have.

The first step for me in my mental wellness journey was asking for help which is promoted in Cherokee culture. I have mentioned before that I endured trauma at different times in my life and developed negative and self-destructive coping skills. So, when I was finally able to see that those ways of coping were actually making my life harder I decided to make a change. But where was I to start? It's not like you can just walk in somewhere and say "Hey I need help learning how to cope with my life in a positive way." But actually, yes you can if you are willing to take the healthy risk and ask for help. There are vast amounts of mental health resources that we can take advantage of depending on your situation. While access may be a barrier to some there are many resources at low or no cost that you can inquire about. Since the beginning of the pandemic, there has been a sharp increase in the number of mental health resources available virtually as well. I am grateful to be living in a time where the stigma of receiving help for mental health is declining. You should not feel ashamed of asking for help or participating in treatment for mental health. Instead, you should be celebrated for being responsible for your own mental wellness and I salute you. This thinking is more in line with traditional Cherokee teachings that promoted mental wellness and the personal responsibility of asking for help when needed.

So what does it mean to be mentally well? For me, mental wellness means I am actively working toward positive outcomes for myself. This means that I am practicing the components of the Walking In Balance program and I view my life in a positive light. This does not mean that I am happy all of the time but that I am balanced. I can cope with adversity and am resilient. I know that wellness may be described as a lack of illness but I believe you can be mentally well even if you have a mental illness. If we continue to grow and work toward positive outcomes and positively view our lives then we are on the right path.

Much of my mental wellness includes prevention and growth. I put in work now and stay ready so that I do not have to get ready should I be faced with adversity. For me, this means talking about my thoughts and feelings and processing them. I do some of this with family and friends but I also go to counseling regularly as it helps to have a trained professional aid me in my mental wellness journey. I also practice self-compassion and self-care so that I can stay balanced and spiritually centered. Next, I do what makes me happy and excited. For me, this usually involves family, sports and practicing Cherokee culture and spirituality. Also, it is important to continue to push yourself to grow and learn new things as well so that we do not become stagnant but continue our ascent toward fulfillment.

Positive Thinking

Negative thoughts were treated with the same care as wounds or physical illness by Cherokee healers because they understood that unchecked negative thinking can manifest itself in our lives. I am aware that positive thinking is not the sole solution to many complex mental wellness issues. However, positive thinking can help you to arrive at a solution faster and help you to enjoy your mental wellness journey more. Our thoughts trigger emotions and feelings and dictate our actions. If we are thinking negatively then we are already manifesting negative results, not to mention taxing our bodies as well. Negative thinking could prevent us from seeking mental health treatment in the first place so it is one of the first things that we should work on. I have heard positive thinking described as "being of good mind" and it has definitely had a profound impact on my life. Much of my negative thinking stems from trauma and other issues but by setting an intention daily I get to determine my focus and can think positively. Positive thinking helps me to reframe my life as the beautiful thing that it is instead of the dreary place that it used to be. It is the same place as before but positive thinking helps me to focus on the good things in the world and in my life. This gives me hope, makes me excited for the future and gives me a boost of energy to complete my work.

In the past, I have often tempered my expectations and not let myself enjoy things or get too excited as a way of protecting myself. When something good happened I wouldn't allow myself to enjoy it for long in case it was taken away. Also, when there was a possibility of failure I would immediately focus on what could go wrong and I never let myself get excited about anything in case it didn't pan out. This defense mechanism protected me from getting let down too much but it also prevented me from experiencing joy or excitement or contentment. So I went through life thinking negatively the majority of the time and guess what? I got negative results from my life a majority of the time. Now, I focus on the positive all of the time. I start my day by practicing gratitude for all of the blessings in my life. I look at situations as challenges now instead of problems and I make a concerted effort not to judge myself or others.

Positive thinking does take practice and it doesn't mean that you will never have a negative thought again. I still have negative thoughts but now I can catch those negative thoughts and change them. For instance, your tire blows out while driving down the road and your first thought could be "great this is going to ruin my day." Now I will catch that thought and I will think "hey you know what this isn't a big deal as I have a spare and I will be back on the road in no time." I may .even challenge myself to see how fast I can change the tire. So, where this situation could have ruined my whole morning, now I see it for the minor inconvenience that it is and move along with having a great day. Also, before I was a big worst-case scenario guy and in any given situation I would often go to the worst thing that could happen. Now, instead of thinking about what is the worst that could happen I focus instead on what is the best that could happen. This thinking helps me to silence my inner critic and take more healthy risks in my personal and professional life and accomplish my goals.

Physical Wellness

Cherokee people put such a high value on physical wellness that we even incorporate it into our ceremonies. When we go to our ceremonial grounds we always play stickball before we eat and dance. I was taught that stickball and fellowship were just as an important part of the ceremony as the singing and dancing were. Stickball involves a lot of running and chasing and laughing and was a way for our people to have fun, settle disputes and maintain our physical wellness. This physical activity was incorporated into our ceremonial life because our ancestors understood the benefits of being physically active while having fun. Stickball teaches several lessons such as the importance of humor, fun, comradery, connection and respect. That is why it has remained such an integral part of our ceremonial life because it is the perfect combination of fun, physical activity and teaching.

My path toward physical wellness changed the day that I began to focus on being happy with myself instead of trying to impress others. Because I had such low self-esteem for much of my life, the need for other people's approval seeped into every facet of my being including how I approached physical wellness. My motivation for engaging in a physical wellness program consisted of wanting to look good to others. So, because my motivation was off I believe that hindered any real progress no matter how much I wanted to be well. It wasn't just my motivation that was lacking, however. Poor time management skills often left me driving through a fast food joint because I always seemed to be late for something. This left me eating a lot of unhealthy food which, in turn, made me too tired to work out even when I did have the time. Also, because I was primarily exercising to please others I was not ever really excited to go work out which meant a lot of fitness programs started but never finished. So, my workouts were sporadic, my eating habits were horrible, my sleep wasn't restful and I just generally felt like crap most of the time.

Another impediment to my being physically well was the fact that I had been a workaholic for several years. I only recently realized this and I just thought that I was being a good provider and a good worker who contributed to the economy. So what if I drop dead from a heart attack in my mid-forties right? It wasn't until the pandemic hit that I feel like people really began to question what was important in life. As Americans, we are expected to be workaholics. We are expected to skip vacation days and work when we are sick and spend more time with our coworkers than we do with our own families. I have seen that meme several times now where it is pointed out how quickly our employers can and will replace us should we pass away. So, I have finally decided to get off of the hamster wheel. I take my breaks now and use my vacation days and sick days. I call off if I need a mental health day and no longer volunteer to take on more than I can handle.

Now that I follow a physical wellness program for my benefit only I stick to it because I am realistic about my abilities and I do what I enjoy. Whereas before I would lift heavy weights and run a lot (I hate running by the way) so that I would look good to others, I now walk more and use lighter weights. For my age, it is recommended that I exercise for 30 minutes 5 out of 7 days. This not only keeps me in shape but makes me feel better. I also completely cut out pop (soda to the non-Okie) and rarely eat fast food. I make sure to drink water and get 8 hours of sleep a night. I know that eating healthy is easier said than done and reading food labels requires a keen eye nowadays because it seems like some food companies try to trick you into believing their product is healthy when it is not. So, to simplify things for myself I really try to eat non-processed food. This means more fruits and vegetables. My diet mostly consists of egg whites or cereal for breakfast, a salad or sandwich for lunch and for dinner $^{1}/_{4}$ protein, $^{1}/_{4}$ starch and $^{1}/_{2}$ of my plate vegetables.

For me, the key to physical wellness is planning. When I make an action plan then I have my meals planned out, I have my exercise time scheduled and I have everything I need to accomplish my goals. When I do not plan then I can end up eating high-calorie comfort food, may skip workouts because of other obligations and can quickly feel unwell with anxiety. So for me, the key is to plan and prep my healthy meals and plan my exercise time. This does not have to be very involved, however, as I know that you are crunched for time as it is. The night before I put my breakfast and lunch into containers so that I can grab them easily on my way to work. This just takes 5 minutes or so. Next, I schedule my physical activity times and if I am busy then I can break up my 30 minutes of daily exercise into 15 or 10-minute increments because something is better than nothing. I know that we feel like we don't have the time but our physical health is worth the work and it really takes a minimal amount of time and planning.

If we do not make time for our physical wellness then we may eventually be forced to take time due to illness. One thing that the pandemic has shown us is that our physical wellness can prevent many serious health complications. So, I had to prioritize my time to make sure that I have time to support my health. It took practice but I now have a routine that I enjoy and makes me feel good. Quitting pop was hard but I used the same principle that I used when I quit drinking alcohol and that made it manageable. One day at a time. I can do anything for one day so when I wanted to quit I would just focus on that day instead of a lifetime which can be overwhelming. I will not drink pop today. I also incorporated physical wellness into my daily affirmations by telling myself that I no longer desire health-destroying junk food and it worked. Of course, I still enjoy comfort food from time to time, in moderation. So, when I do eat some junk food I get to enjoy it because I know that I eat healthy for the majority of the time so I do not need to feel guilty. This is what works for me but I encourage you to make a physical wellness plan that works for you. I would like to mention that going to regular checkups and attending all of your appointments is also practicing physical wellness. I used to skip appointments because I did not want to hear bad news but now I am happy to go and ensure that I am doing everything I can to keep my body healthy. If there is an issue I am more likely to catch it early if I am getting checkups regularly and can then get any necessary treatment. I now take responsibility for my own health and am much happier for it.

Social Wellness

I mentioned before that balance and wellness were central to Cherokee cultural teachings and that is also true when it comes to our relationships. Social wellness means that we have healthy and positive connections with the people in our life. Traditionally, Cherokee people had unique family and social systems that were practical and served a purpose. For instance, since we were a matrilineal tribe, children were often very close to their mother's brothers. There were several reasons for this but one was that if something happened to your father you would still have your uncles to guide you. This was true for me as my uncles taught me much of what being a strong Cherokee man entailed. I was taught about respect, perseverance and forgiveness. However, there are also lessons to be learned from those relationships we choose. Like our family, our friendships should be rooted in mutual respect and provide support and help us to cope with life's changes. Take a look at your relationships. Do the people in your life support you? Do your relationships bring you positivity and strength and belonging? If not then it may be time to consider changing who you associate with or at the very least establish some boundaries. However, if you want to be socially well then it begins with ensuring that you have a positive relationship with yourself. I have battled with social anxiety at different times in my life but have persevered and now I have positive relationships that bring value to my life. The goal is to have positive social interactions with everyone in our lives whether they are family, friends or acquaintances.

In the past, I have struggled with social wellness as my interactions with friends, family and peers were not always positive. It was hard to have positive interactions when I had low self-esteem, no self-respect and poor communication skills. Also, because of my limited communication skills, I always found most social interactions to be exhausting. I have been socially awkward for as long as I remember. If you go to shake my hand I will probably try to high-five you. I am a little awkward when around new people but that is ok. I am not a big fan of a lot of eye contact (it's a cultural thing) and small talk feels like a bunch of tiny needles being stabbed into my brain. In my youth it was hard for me at times to keep up with conversations with my peers and jokes would often go over my head. I would just smile and nod though because I really didn't care to find out the punchline. I think the worst time for me was when the teacher or professor would say "let's break into groups and discuss this topic further." I have tried at times to be super social and would approach people to form a group and try hard to be talkative but I hated it. Other times I would just wander around the room until everyone but the awkwards were left and we would form our own little awkward group. The funny thing is, though, that in the awkward group I was always elected the spokesperson.

Things definitely began to change for me once I began working on self-acceptance and mindfulness. The whole time I was trying to fit in with the witty, good looking and really intense eye contact group and I wasn't that. So, instead, I started focusing on accepting myself more and the doors finally began to unlock for me. Now I accept and love myself and am realistic about my abilities and limitations. I still do not think group work with strangers and small talk is the funnest thing in the world but I enjoy it a lot more than I used to and I often find productive conversations after the initial awkwardness is over. I can confidently hold my own in any social setting because I do not have to prove anything to anyone. I now know who I am and that person is pretty awesome. What I have to say has value and I am happy to share what I know and also learn from others.

Another component of social wellness once you get past the small talk is our relationships themselves. Do you have positive relationships? Do you know how to have a positive relationship? For me, this has been a struggle at times also. You see, I never really had any intention when choosing who I formed relationships with and it was usually out of shared interests that I befriended people. So, when I wasn't feeling well and was making poor decisions then I gravitated toward other people who were doing the same. The people that we associate with are often a reflection of how we feel about ourselves and how we treat ourselves provides others with the template for how we should be treated. If we treat ourselves poorly then it may signal to others that it is okay for them to treat us poorly as well.

So I believe that for us to be socially well it starts with working on ourselves first. Learning to accept and love ourselves will enable us to be confident in any social setting because we no longer feel the need to be someone else or try to impress others. You do not need the validation of others to feel confident and happy. Also, make sure you communicate with yourself in a positive way by using positive self-talk. Social connection is very important as isolation puts you at risk for physical and mental health issues as well as substance abuse. As we continue to work on our self-acceptance and confidence through affirmations and other activities we can then establish what we want from our relationships. Social wellness means that we have supportive people in our life who respect our boundaries. So, it is important to establish what your values are, how you want to be treated and what you are comfortable with. As we continue to practice self-acceptance and our confidence begins to grow then we can be assertive in our relationships and enforce our boundaries.

Action Steps

Set an intention daily

It helps me to set an intention daily to maintain my focus on wellness. After my gratitude exercises and a quiet minute of self-reflection, I set an intention to work on or focus on one, two or three areas that I feel need attention.

Examine old coping/survival skills

For those of us who experienced trauma in our youth, we may have developed negative coping or survival skills that no longer serve us. One awesome thing about growth is that we can change the way that we do things whenever we want. One survival skill that I developed in my youth that no longer serves me is isolation. I erected emotional walls in my youth to prevent myself from being hurt and this did help me cope at the time. However, this coping skill also served to keep me disconnected from others and left me feeling lonely. So, I began the work of letting this coping skill go and replacing it with one that serves me and my current lifestyle much better.

Keep a journal for mental wellness

This has helped me in the past to keep track of my intentions and progress. I like to be reminded of my accomplishments and areas that may require a little more focus. Also, I have found that journaling or talk therapy helps me to process my thoughts and emotions better than just trying to hash them out in my head.

Positive affirmations

I talked about positive affirmations before but I cannot overstate their importance in my wellness regimen as they improve many facets of my life.

Practice Mindfulness

Practicing mindfulness regularly has improved all aspects of my wellness. It helps my mental wellness by slowing my thoughts down so that I do not get overwhelmed. Practicing mindfulness also helps me to process my thoughts and emotions.

Give yourself space to process emotions and communicate them

It is no secret that we are very busy every day and it is possible to be walking around with feelings and emotions that are not aware of. I have often suppressed or ignored my feelings because who has the time to deal with them right? Unfortunately, that is not a very good solution for me because when I do not take time to acknowledge and process my feelings and emotions then they are often manifested in unpleasant ways. As I mentioned, I went to visit a family member awhile back who is very ill and did not think anything of it. Later, when I returned home, my spouse noticed that I was in a bad mood and asked me what the matter was. I sat and thought for a minute and realized that I wasn't angry, I was sad about my visit. However, I am so used to running from one event to another that I sometimes neglect to check in with myself and process my emotions. Now, I am more mindful of my emotions and make sure to check in with myself regularly. Then, I make sure to give myself space to process my emotions by talking with someone or practicing mindfulness.

Exercise & Eat healthy

I know that you have been preached to a lot about the benefits of getting your recommended amount of daily exercise and eating a healthy diet. So, the only advice I will give on this subject is to be compassionate with yourself during your physical wellness journey. Start with small goals that are manageable and create a routine that you enjoy and that fits into your schedule. This makes it more likely that you will stick with your routine and find sustained success.

Get 8 hours of sleep

I know that many of us need more restful sleep and I also know that it is easier said than done. There are many reasons why we are often not able to get 8 hours of restful sleep. Anxiety, stress and an overwhelming schedule can all prevent us from resting as we should. However, there are many tools that you can use to enable yourself to get better rest. For instance, where before I would work all the way until bedtime I now shut things down and make sure that I have time before bed to relax and unwind. Part of that includes doing my "what went well" list. This just involves me recalling everything during the day that went well instead of worrying about what I didn't get done or any mistakes I made. Next, I turn off my phone so that I am not worried about it going off in the middle of the night. Last, I have a pre-bedtime ritual that involves practicing self-compassion, practicing deep breathing and giving myself permission to rest after a long day's work.

Establish boundaries in relationships and say "no" when you need time for yourself

For some people establishing healthy boundaries is easy and saying "no" to others is easy. However, for recovering people-pleasers such as myself, this can be very hard. In the past, I really needed people to like me as that was the source of much of my self-worth. However, as my self-worth is now derived internally, I now feel more comfortable establishing and enforcing healthy boundaries. Also, sometimes I am tired and I need rest. I have been warned in the past about "burning the candle at both ends" and have learned that I must make time for rest and self-care. So, now I make sure to enforce my boundaries and if people cannot respect my boundaries then I limit the amount of time that I spend with them. I also say "no" now if I need time to rest or recuperate and I no longer feel bad about it. The fact of the matter is that I cannot expect other people to put my health and well-being first and I must take on the personal responsibility of doing that and am much happier and healthier for it.

Sobriety

ᎣᏓᏅᏗᏌᏅ
Odanvtisanv

We aspire to practice active sobriety in order to live a vibrant and fulfilling life.

There is a reason why Cherokee ceremonial grounds forbid alcohol on the premises. When you put a substance into your body like alcohol or other drugs it numbs your senses and creates a barrier to spiritual connection. So, if you are not connected with your spirit then it is difficult to Walk In Balance and realize your full potential. Using drugs or alcohol is not even an effective way to cope because whatever problems you need help coping with will not be helped by you avoiding them. Also, whatever issues you are having will likely be made worse by alcohol and drug use. This is very important to remember for those who are most at risk for substance abuse. So, the best thing would be for us to never start using drugs or alcohol as a means of coping because there is a chance that you will be that person who becomes an addict or alcoholic. Unfortunately, I have known several people who have passed away due to substance abuse.

There are many reasons why alcohol and drugs are an ineffective means of coping. This has been my experience as alcohol and drugs only exacerbated the issues that I was trying to cope with. I began using alcohol because I sought relief from my anxiety and to cope with trauma but any perceived relief was short-lived. I always felt worse after the alcohol wore off and so naturally I would start drinking again so that I would feel better. This started a dangerous cycle for me early on in life and it almost killed me. I have several friends and family members who were killed by their addictions so I now try to warn others about the dangers of using alcohol and drugs as a way to cope. I had many people throughout my life tell me not to do drugs. I remember school presentations, commercials and respected adults telling me about the dangers of using drugs. However, I only remember one person telling me that I shouldn't drink. That person also had a beer in their hand when passing along this sage advice so it was kind of a conflicted message. Youth may not always do what you say but they will often do what you do so the best way to teach something is to model it yourself.

I feel as though many of us are deceived by alcohol because it is widely accepted and in the beginning, many are unaware of the dangers that lie at the bottom of the bottle. Alcohol commercials always feature attractive people who are smiling and having a great time but that was never my experience. Everyone I knew drank for effect and the scene instead often involved people laughing, then crying, then fighting. Instead of smiling people dancing there were often busted windows and run-ins with the police. So, when I started experiencing negative effects because of my alcohol use I didn't think anything of it because everyone I knew drank like that. I began my drinking career in my teenage years as a way to find acceptance with others and I also wanted to feel better. Alcohol gave me a false sense of confidence and I thought that I had found a wonder drug. When I drank I was more outgoing and personable and it allowed me to block out and forget about the pain and problems in my life. Of course, that feeling was short-lived and was replaced by anger and then anxiety and shame as the alcohol left my body. When I was young, many people talked about marijuana as a gateway drug that would lead to all sorts of other substance abuse but me for it was alcohol.

I feel like the only thing that kept me from drinking a lot in my teenage years was my sporadic access to it. Had it been more accessible I would have partaken much more than I did. Of course that all changed when I turned 21 and could drink any time that I wanted. The next 11 years were a continuous cycle of employment, excessive drinking, loss of employment, family problems resulting from my drinking, apologies from me and a vow to do better; then repeat. Though I drank to cope with life's challenges I just ended up creating more challenges for myself when I drank but my pickled mind could not see that. Alcohol wasn't the problem, it was my boss and my family and everything and everyone in the world. Or so I thought. I do not need to talk at length about my drinking and drugging career as it is a familiar one that many know all too well. Suffice it to say that by the end I was suicidal and often prayed for death just so I could be released from the bondage of self-loathing and self-pity. I drank every day from the moment I woke up to the moment I went to sleep just so I wouldn't get ill or have seizures and I was sick and tired of being sick and tired. It had gotten so bad that I couldn't remember how to tie my shoes and I really felt like death was near.

My friend John Aaron once told me that when it gets hard enough then you will make a change. Well, it was finally hard enough and so I checked myself into a drug and alcohol treatment center with the help of the Torres Martinez Tribe. The rehabilitation center was located in the middle of the desert and it was August and the temperature was regularly over 110 degrees. My first few days were a blur as I began going through withdrawal from alcohol. I just remember shivering a lot even though it was hot and there were flies everywhere. I felt like a character in One Flew Over the Cuckoo's Nest and only stayed because there was another addict there who talked me out of leaving for three days straight. Oh yeah, and the fact that I was miles from town and would have certainly died walking in the heat was another incentive to stay. I was at the rehabilitation center for three days when I finally started to see a ray of hope.

I was sitting under a tree outside one morning when I had what alcoholics refer to as a moment of clarity. I remember seeing a bright light and a feeling of warmth came over me. I was not alarmed because hallucinations were not uncommon toward the end of my drinking and during the withdrawal period. But this was different. I believe it was a spirit. My spirit. I made a decision right then and there that I would give everything I had in order to get sober and if I was indeed going to die soon then I would die sober. I was going to make myself proud. I finally had hope. It was faint, like a glimmer in the dark but I began to nurture the hope that change was possible. I became a man on fire and started to soak up any and all information that could help me maintain my sobriety and respect myself again. It turns out that I program well which is kind of sad because I had a lot of practice. From the Indian boarding school as a child to drug treatment and emotional growth schools as a teen to jail to more treatment centers as an adult, I had a lot of experience. However, I used this to my advantage and began to work a recovery program that I still work to this day. It is amazing what we can accomplish when we set our intention and believe in ourselves.

I share this because there is a high incidence of alcohol use in the United States and many people die each year due to substance abuse. For many, this is a generational curse that continues to perpetuate historical trauma and wreak havoc on our communities. This is especially true during the pandemic as many more people have turned to drugs and alcohol as a way to cope with the stress. However, there is a better way. I remember when I was still drinking and I would hear people talk about being high on life. I wanted to throw something at them but it was because they had something that I desperately wanted. They could cope and enjoy life without having to drink or use drugs. Back then I thought that it was just biology. Those people were better than me as I was born flawed. I felt as though there was nothing I could do to change my situation but of course, I was wrong.

Early in recovery, I began to reflect on the spiritual and cultural teachings that elders tried to convey in my youth. I began to practice those teachings again and was happy to find that I began to feel better than I had ever felt but it depended on the amount of work that I was willing to put in. I had to abandon my previous coping skills and work on my defense mechanisms that kept me isolated and convinced that I was unworthy of love. Now all these years later life just keeps getting better because I am willing to put in the work every day. Of course, my life isn't perfect and I still have adversity from time to time but now I see any issues that arise as challenges instead of problems and I try to see what I can learn from any experience. Practicing active sobriety helps me to stay present and patient as I continue my journey through life. I learn more every day which is awesome because you never know what life is going to bring but when I am sober then no matter what challenges I face I still remember that every day is a good day.

Action Steps

Ask for help

I would like to help normalize asking for help. I know that rugged individualism is promoted heavily in many sectors of American society but this is not a traditional Indigenous concept. Native people have always believed that we can accomplish more by working together and helping one another. So, it would be beneficial for us to dispel the myth that we are supposed to have the ability to be successful on our own. The fact of the matter is that historical trauma is still very prevalent in our communities and we need to help one another to find ways to cope in healthy ways and not resort to using drugs or alcohol. However, we cannot be expected to receive help if we are not ready to leave behind the old patterns that bring misery to our lives. If we are ready to try a new and positive way of living, though, then we can expect assistance along the way. We won't find out unless we take the healthy risk and ask.

Identify triggers

If you are struggling to stay sober then it helps to identify situations that make you want to drink. This could be people, places or things. For instance, payday was a trigger for me because I was used to drinking on Fridays as a way to socialize with others. Of course, the trouble was that I would continue drinking long after everyone else had stopped. Another trigger for me was stress. Due to my limited coping skills, I would become overwhelmed with anxiety when I had stressors occur in my life. So I would be triggered to drink in order to quell the symptoms of my anxiety. Any relief was short-lived, however, as the drinking only served to make my situation worse. I couldn't even listen to country music for the first few years that I was sober because it triggered a response in me that made me want to drink. I know that many of you may feel that country music would make anyone want to drink but I associated it with alcohol. So, once you can identify your triggers it makes it easier to avoid those situations and develop a plan and positive coping skills to help you overcome your triggers.

Develop a list of positive ways to cope with stress and anxiety

There are so many better ways to cope with anxiety and stress than alcohol or drugs. Unfortunately, when we begin to experience symptoms of stress, anxiety and trauma we are often taught that drinking alcohol is a socially acceptable way to manage those symptoms. We may even be taught by others that using drugs is the best way to cope. However, although counseling, practicing mindfulness and talking about your feelings may take a little patience to see results, it is a far better way to cope. If we have a list of positive coping skills ready then we will be much better suited to handle life's ups and downs effectively.

Make a plan for when you are triggered to drink or use drugs

Once we have identified our triggers and have made a list of positive ways to cope then we can make a plan of action. This really requires minimal time and effort especially compared to the misery that coping with drugs and alcohol can bring. It helps to have a plan for when you are triggered to use so that you feel more prepared for life and are less likely to become so overwhelmed that you are tempted to cope in negative ways.

Practice Walking In Balance and healthy living daily

I believe that the best way to cope and thrive despite any circumstance is prevention. I know that everyone is so busy that you may feel like a lot of days you are playing catch up or are merely surviving. However, it is my hope that we all begin to take back control over our lives. We get to decide how we want to feel each day. We get to set our schedule. So, it helps to incorporate the Walking In Balance teachings into your daily/weekly/monthly schedule so that you can break out of the over-stress and anxiety cycle. This may require you to set some boundaries and make some decisions about what your priorities are but the effort is so worth the results.

Avoid people/situations that trigger an urge to use

Speaking of boundaries. Sometimes we have to make the decision to spend less time with those who aren't supportive of our wellness journey. Someone once told me that I have to take care of myself before I can take care of anyone else, especially if that person isn't ready to live a healthy lifestyle and make positive choices. Nothing changes if nothing changes right? So, sometimes we have to take the healthy risk to put ourselves and our wellness first to change things in our lives. You will be surprised by how much one person getting sober can positively change a family and a community. If you are struggling with substance abuse just know that many people have stood where you are now and a beautiful life awaits in sobriety.

Respect

ᏗᏓᏓᏂᎸᏍᏗ
Didadanilvsdi

We aspire to always show respect to ourselves, others and the environment.

Cherokee people place a high value on respect. In our youth, we are taught to respect elders because of the work they have done on our behalf and the knowledge that they keep. We are taught to respect ourselves by treating ourselves well and acting per our values. We are taught to respect others by treating them how they want to be treated without judgment. Cherokee people also believe that we are only a small part of the earth and we have a responsibility to care for the animals and the environment. Our survival depends on us to be able to coexist in harmony and balance so respect for the environment is also very important.

Respect for Self

There are several variations of the definition of self-respect but many include pride, confidence, dignity and integrity. For much of my life, I lacked self-respect and often confused self-respect with self-esteem or ego. I did not treat myself with respect or respect the person that I saw in the mirror. I also suffered from low self-esteem and did not have much confidence in my abilities. So, I often countered those feelings of inadequacy with an inflated ego. I knew that I wanted to feel better and have more confidence but did not have the tools at the moment so I would often exaggerate my importance and abilities to feel like I was on a level playing field with everyone else. Since I did not feel equal to others I often felt the need to brag about myself and play up my importance to prove to others that I was confident. Of course, that was not the case and often when I was alone I was left feeling empty and inadequate.

This went on for much of my life and looking back now I am proud of everything that I accomplished without many of the necessary skills to fully practice wellness. I was taught a lot about respecting others and the environment but I was not able to connect with all of the lessons and stories about self-respect that elders tried to convey. I remember the first time I saw someone with healthy emotional boundaries and I was blown away. Healthy boundaries? What a nerd. However, that moment stuck with me for a long time because I wanted that. I needed that in my life but it would be a little while before I had the tools to work on my self-respect. The lack of respect for myself also contributed to my feelings of being an imposter. Because I did lack self-confidence I never really felt like I belonged anywhere. I often felt like a fraud when I would try new things or try to push myself to take healthy risks in athletics, academics and social settings. Because I felt like I had to pretend to be something that I wasn't I couldn't realistically assess my skillset so even when I did find success in any area I would often attribute it to luck instead of my own efforts. These feelings and my lack of self-respect ultimately led me to find acceptance among those who felt just as bad as I did and thus began my era of self-medicating. I am grateful that I just didn't accept this way of life forever but instead found tools to increase my self-respect.

I am proud to say that I now respect myself and treat myself with respect. Even though I respect myself today I know that could change if I fall back into old patterns. Just like everything else I have to put in the work to maintain my self-respect but it is so worth the effort. My journey toward self-respect started with defining what I was about. Who am I? What do I really believe in? What are my strengths and weaknesses? Once I was able to articulate who I was, what my values were and what I was capable of then I could start to understand the person in the mirror. This required a lot of self-reflection which I had been pushed to do for much of my life by elders and therapists but I finally knew what I was looking for. Whereas, before I felt like I was trying to find a light switch in the dark I now at least had some tools to help me.

I began by describing myself unabashedly and was pleasantly surprised when I looked at the collection of words on the paper. Loving, caring, helpful, intelligent, strong, forgiving, and powerful. These were just some of the words that came from the exercise and for the first time in my life I didn't try to qualify these descriptions at all. I claimed them instead. Yes, I am all of those things! Moreover, I am worthy and a survivor and I love and respect myself. Yes, I have made mistakes in my life but as Maya Angelou said, "Do the best you can until you know better. Then when you know better, do better." That is all we can do. So, I forgive myself for the past because I did the best that I could and now that I know better I get to do better. After I started to get reacquainted with who I was I also wrote down a list of what I believed in.

What values are important to me? Not give a like on Facebook important but I will live my life by them important. Honesty, service, sobriety, respect and all of the components of the Walking In Balance program are included in that list. Now I have a framework for how I want to live my life and a reference point for where my boundaries need to be. Well, look at me! I get to be a nerdy guy with healthy boundaries! I am really amazed sometimes that I survived without this for much of my life because without articulating my values the wind could really blow me in any direction.

The next thing that I did was take an honest look at what my strengths and weaknesses were. It is important to know what you are good at, what areas you can improve upon and what you like to do or you may end up hamstrung by doing work that isn't suited for you and you dislike. This is easy enough to do if you are able to be honest about your abilities and preferences. However, for much of my life, I made decisions based off of what I thought others wanted out of me instead of what I wanted for myself. Now, I can be authentic and this has improved my confidence tremendously.

We respect ourselves by making sure that we are consuming only what will build our strength and keep us healthy. From the food we eat to the information that we are consuming, it is important to limit our intake of negativity. It is also important to act within our values so that we do not lose respect for ourselves along the way. Last, we show respect for ourselves when we acknowledge that our self-worth should not be dictated by external forces. We are worthy and deserve respect just because of who we are. So, remind yourself often that you are worthy of love and respect no matter your profession, size, age or ability. I only mention this because I made the mistake of connecting my self-worth and self-respect to my job. I only felt like I deserved respect as long as I made a certain amount of money and had a certain position. This belief kept me stagnant as I was afraid to take healthy risks and chase my dreams because I wasn't sure who I was without that job. So, speaking from experience, it is beneficial to love and respect yourself for who you are and not what you do or how you look because those things will eventually change. However, you can be a person of integrity that is worthy and respected forever.

Respect for Others

Cherokee people believe that respect for others helps us to maintain balance in our homes, communities and environment. Treat others how you would like to be treated. I heard this often in school as a child. However, this thinking has evolved as of late to instead dictate that we treat others how they want to be treated. This is more in line with Cherokee customs as everyone is different and has different feelings about things. This does take a little more work as we have to be aware of how others want to be treated and respect their boundaries. However, this little bit of work can yield extremely positive results in our homes and communities. A great mentor of mine, Robert Friedman, helped me to understand how respect and kindness can restore balance in our lives and the lives of others.

There are many ways to show respect for others but I would like to highlight a few that I practice and that have helped me foster positive relationships. First, I show respect to others without judgment. I don't care what you look like or where you are from. I show respect to everyone and by doing this I not only respect the other person but I show respect to myself by acting within my values. Also, I believe that by respecting our differences I allow for opportunities for growth and education. Next, I show respect for other people's opinions and practice empathy toward others. For much of my life, I felt pressured to always have the right answer and know everything. However, by listening to and acknowledging others, it helps them feel validated and I learn a lot in the process. This fosters positive connections and collaboration in my home and community. I heard somewhere that "I" can accomplish a lot but "we" can accomplish anything and I definitely agree.

The last two things that I would like to mention about respecting others are empathy and gossip. Empathy, yes. Gossip, no. Practicing empathy not only helps others but myself as well as I am often able to avoid miscommunication or aggravation because I better understand where others are coming from. Everyone is tired and everyone gets overwhelmed and we are doing the best that we can in troubling times. Putting yourself in other people's shoes will help you to better understand

and relate to others. This helps us to forgive easier and promotes compassion.

Last, I would like for us all to be the place where gossip goes to die. Gossip has no value in our homes, workplaces and communities as it hinders respect and connection. I have been guilty of gossiping in the past as I was still in the chaos and drama cycle but in order to maintain peace within and show respect for others, I had to quit the cycle. I know gossip is addicting as you want to be in on the gossip instead of being the one people are talking about but it only hurts others and your own self-respect as well. Also, I finally realized that instead of trying to bring others down to make myself feel better I should instead focus on myself and lift myself up. Now, if I know someone is having a hard time I will pray for them instead of talking about them. If I am in company that is gossiping I will politely address the group and let people know that I am uncomfortable with it. However, if you want to avoid direct confrontation you can either change the subject or say something nice about the target of the gossip. I have done both and it quickly changes the conversation to a more positive and supportive tone.

Respect for the Environment

Cherokees, like many Native people, have historically shown respect for the environment by practicing eco-friendly living. Though this is often seen as a progressive stance, Cherokees have been living this way since time immemorial. Cherokee people believe that by showing respect for the environment then we will be able to live in balance and harmony for years to come. However, we have begun to witness the effects of what happens when that balance is disrupted. Ecological disasters such as animal extinction and pollution of air and water are just a few instances of this. Native people have continued to lead the way when it comes to respecting the environment as evidenced by protections for endangered species and our natural resources. Unfortunately, Native people are not always consulted when decisions are being made about how to protect the environment. However, we can all take steps in our daily living to help reduce our impact on our environment.

So how do we go about saving the planet? First, it helped me to understand that I cannot do it alone, today. Though I was tempted to go off-grid and live in a cabin in the woods forever swearing off the trappings of modern society, I remembered that I could just incorporate respect for the environment into my daily living. That being said, the cabin idea is not entirely off the table. In the meantime, however, I began to examine my life for ways to reduce my imprint on the environment and improve my community. So, I began to make small changes in my life that I felt would meet that goal. Where available I try to take public transportation as much as possible, I recycle and try to be mindful of waste when purchasing and I look for opportunities to volunteer in my community. Cherokee people are also taught to give something back to the earth when we harvest something as a way to show respect, gratitude and maintain balance with our environment.

This issue has been politicized over the years but the fact is that we all share responsibility for our environment. I often spend time in nature as a way to practice spiritual wellness and if our environment is unwell then we will be unwell also. However, I also know from experience that it can be overwhelming trying to change everything at once which may end up just making you quit. So, I recommend looking for ways to make small changes in your life to reduce your impact on the environment and help bring balance back to our communities. Maybe you start a recycling program at school or install eco-friendly shower heads at home or volunteer to clean up local waterways. The point is that we can all do something and if we all work together then all of those little things can make a big difference for our environment.

Action Steps

Determine your values

I know that most of us do not have a list of family values on our wall alongside a family crest. However, it has been extremely helpful for me to determine what my values are. Once I know what values I want to live my life by then I can set boundaries in my life because I know what direction I am heading and what I will and will not tolerate.

Act within your values

This continues to be one of the best ways to maintain my self-respect and also helps me stay out of drama. I respect the person that I am today because I work hard to ensure that I live my life in accordance with my values. I am not perfect and I still make mistakes, however, since I work on myself regularly my mistakes are on a much smaller scale than before. Also, if I make a mistake or unintentionally hurt someone's feelings then

I make sure to promptly apologize if warranted which also helps me to maintain my self-respect and inner peace.

Change negative thoughts

Changing our negative thoughts and negative self-talk enables us to change the narrative of our lives. This is important because it is hard to respect the person we see in the mirror if we continue to think negative thoughts about that person. So, by practicing self-compassion we can forgive ourselves for our mistakes and change how we talk to ourselves. Then when our negative thoughts come we can catch them and change them to positive thoughts about ourselves and our situation.

Spend time with respectful people

It is hard to continue to stay positive and respectful to yourself and others if you are consistently subjected to negativity and disrespect. What we consume influences our thoughts so if we are hearing negativity and disrespect regularly then it is harder to maintain a positive outlook that is conducive to living a life of respect.

Treat others how they want to be treated

It is well-intentioned to treat others how we want to be treated but if we take just a little time to make ourselves aware of how others want to be treated then that fosters respect. The fact of the matter is that we are all different so by treating others how they want to be treated then we are showing them through our actions that they are valued.

Treat animals and the environment with respect

I was told a story when I was young about spirits that would punish you if you were mean to animals. Many lessons in Cherokee culture were often conveyed through storytelling and it is because Cherokee people believe that everything is connected. Therefore, by treating animals and the environment with respect then I am respecting myself as well. There are many different ways to practice this action step. From volunteering at a local animal shelter to recycling to picking up trash in our communities, there are endless ways for us to support our environment and all of its inhabitants.

Communication

ᏗᏓᏛᎪᏙᏗ
Didadvgododi

We aspire to communicate effectively and practice active listening.

Much of what I learned about communicating effectively was when I was young and I would watch elders speak to each other. I remember that whether the words were spoken in Cherokee or English there was a rhythm to the words and nobody was in a hurry. When I would go with my uncle to visit people I remember there was a ritual to the visit that was almost always followed. First, the television was turned off and coffee was put on and the children would often go outside to play as the adults spoke. Another thing that I notice now that I look back on those memories is that people spoke carefully, clearly and really listened to each other. Nobody ever spoke over each other during these conversations and people often took a moment or two before they responded. This allowed the speaker to add anything if they wished and it gave the listener time to process what was being said before they responded. Of course, not every conversation is this structured but it is a good model to follow when communicating. We will have a lot more success if we are a little more considerate when we speak to each other.

It is important to work on your communication so that you can effectively communicate your needs to others. Cherokee people have always understood that it is important to communicate with others how we are doing so that we don't get built up with negative thoughts. It is also important to communicate your emotions in order to maintain balance and stay connected to those around you. I like to communicate about everything no matter if I am having a good day or if I am facing adversity. Communicating gratitude and positivity helps those in your life know that they are valued. Also, letting others in when you are having a tough time builds trust and helps you to process what is going on. I am grateful that I can communicate when I am having anxious thoughts because it helps me to realize how ridiculous they often are. I believe that it is important for people to communicate their feelings so that negative consequences do not occur. I have seen often where it is more acceptable for someone to yell or punch a wall instead of talking about what is bothering them and letting others in. This is something that we have to change so that people know that their feelings are important and that what they have to say has value.

Effective communication means that the message we are trying to convey is understood and we understand what others are communicating to us. While this seems like a very straightforward topic, communicating effectively is actually quite nuanced and at times complicated. In hindsight, I realize now that many of the problems that I encountered in relationships could have been due to my lack of communication skills. There are a variety of factors that hinder our ability to communicate effectively such as not sending a clear or accurate message, communicating while stressed or making assumptions about what the message really is. We also have to be mindful of what we are hearing and practice active listening in order to be respectful of the speaker and allow ourselves the opportunity to accurately receive the message.

Communication styles vary depending on region and culture but that barrier need not hinder us if we set our intention on being understood. No matter what we are communicating I believe it all boils down to what our intentions are. One of my goals when communicating is that my words only be used to lift up others and make sure my needs are met.

It has taken a lot of practice to get better at this and I am proud of the work that I have done up to this point. For much of my life, I was not careful with my words and did not understand the power that they have. I was careless with this power and never thought about how I made others feel when communicating. I would say a lot of inaccurate things that did not serve me or the person that I was communicating with and a lot of that had to do with pain and impatience. I have since been able to work through many of the barriers that kept me from communicating effectively.

I have reexamined how I communicate and I realized that I was doing several things that hampered my ability to communicate effectively and make sure that my needs are met. I remember having a bad day or not feeling well and just looking at my spouse waiting for her to say the right thing to make me feel better as if she was telepathic and could read my mind. This was due to me being out of practice when it came to expressing my emotions and asking for what I needed. I would often just stay in my head and sulk because of my inability to communicate what

I was feeling. It is hard to be real and you have to be willing to take that healthy risk and put yourself out there. However, the alternative is to constantly be frustrated and feel isolated. So, I choose to put myself out there now and be real but there are several steps to this process.

I had the advantage, or some would say disadvantage, of attending an emotional growth boarding school in my teen years. I learned a lot about communicating my feelings but I didn't make much progress because I could not let down my walls and be real. However, when I did let myself experience and communicate my emotions, I felt a lot better. I felt like that young boy again at the Stomp Ground. I felt good about myself and my burden felt lighter because I shared it with others. These moments were few and far between in my younger years though they occur more frequently now that I have set an intention to be real and communicate in a real way. I have a good friend named John Aaron who has always pushed me to communicate in a real and authentic way. He taught me that you have to practice having real conversations and made me see that I was using my words to make others feel not good enough so that I could feel better about myself. He also taught me that there is no perfect way to do it but by communicating with others we can find out what is good about ourselves.

After I set an intention to be real and communicate what I am feeling then I had to practice it. John often tells me about sitting on beaches in different countries where he has real conversations with strangers. I bet it is mind-blowing for a lot of people because John is pretty intense but if you talk to him then you will really get an opportunity to get in touch with your emotions and what is really going on inside you. I admire that and have set out to practice all that I have learned about communicating effectively in order to feel better and make sure my needs are met. First, though I have to be clear about what I am trying to communicate and for me it starts with my family. I make sure to communicate with my children now in a more real and clear way. I want us to be able to talk about our feelings and thoughts. I did not grow up in a very affectionate household and I often was left guessing about how people felt about me. I do not want people in my life to also be unclear about how I feel so I tell my family that I love them a lot. This takes practice and it does get uncomfortable sometimes but we make a little more progress every day and my relationships with those I love are much stronger because of it. I love having real conversations with my kids because they get to communicate how they feel and it helps them process.

Communicating While Stressed or Upset

The first suggestion for this topic is Don't Do It! Seems pretty simple right? Not really because when we are upset that is often the time that we feel the need to communicate the most right? We feel the need to communicate our frustration in order to be rid of it. However, more often than not we usually just end up stressing out those around us and exacerbate the situation. I do not like to communicate when I am very stressed if I can avoid it because there is a greater chance for miscommunication and misunderstanding. I know that when I am stressed I am not thinking as clearly as I would like so my message and delivery can easily be misunderstood. There is also a greater chance of saying something that you don't mean and will have to apologize for later so if at all possible I will pause a conversation and come back to it.

Life happens right? It isn't always pretty as disagreements will happen from time to time and it is important to have a tool kit that we can rely on. When I feel that I am too upset to communicate effectively I will often excuse myself by saying "can you give me a minute to process and we can finish this discussion in a bit?" This gives me time to get my emotions under control so that I can communicate more clearly. I may take a walk or meditate or even take a shower to relax a bit and calm down. The next thing I stay mindful of is to not place blame but instead communicate how I am feeling. So that may look like "it made me sad when this happened" or "I feel that this is the best course to follow." I first try to own my own stuff and communicate it in a way that is heard. I have learned that just saying "you do this" and "you always do that" turns people off and creates a barrier to communicating effectively.

The next tool in my kit is empathy. When I am in a serious discussion I always try to see things from the other person's perspective. That helps me to better understand what is being communicated and often helps me to arrive at solutions quicker. Speaking of solutions, I try to always be mindful of what my intention is when communicating. Do I want to be right, be heard or be effective? If I just want to be right then that means that the other person has to be wrong and things are rarely that cut and dry. So, sometimes it is enough to be heard so that I feel like my feelings are valid even though we may not arrive at a solution right at that moment. Or do I want to be effective? In any relationship or partnership, this is my primary goal. So I pull out another tool in my communication tool kit which is compromise. In my earlier years, I often looked at communication as a competition and I viewed my relationships the same way. Because I had suffered trauma at an early age I developed this survival skill where I had to be hyper-vigilant even when communicating. This survival skill no longer serves me and I know that I am safe in my relationships so I do not have to be on guard anymore and can find solutions where everyone wins. Compromise has helped me to accept that it is okay to not get your way all the time and we truly win as a family.

Action Steps

Communicate honestly

Communicating honestly with others promotes connection because it fosters trust. Also, communicating honestly helps you to maintain your self-respect because you are acting within your values.

Take your time when communicating

This is an action step that I continue to work on. When I am excited I have a tendency to talk over others but now that I am aware of it I try to stay mindful when I am excited to share something. Practicing patience in communication ensures that I effectively communicate my message so that I am understood instead of focusing on the instant gratification of sharing my story. Also, by being patient while communicating I am showing respect to whomever I am communicating with.

Avoid assumptions

There are many variations of a saying that goes something like "a little knowledge is a dangerous thing." This original quote is from the 1700s but referred to the pitfalls of thinking you are an expert in something because you know a little about it. I believe that this can also be applied to our communication when we make assumptions about how we think other people feel or what they are saying. For instance, if your spouse is short with you or has a certain facial expression it is tempting to assume they are in a bad mood or are being disrespectful. I have made this mistake in the past and it is a lot easier to use my words and make further inquiries if I need additional information instead of thinking that I know what is going on just based on a look or tone. This can save us from miscommunication and stress. It is also helpful to remember that all information that we take in gets filtered through our past experiences, trauma and biases so it is helpful to ask for clarification at times.

Avoid blame in conversations

There is nothing more detrimental to us being effective communicators than being accusatory. In my experience blaming others only serves to put them on the defense and it inhibits progress and the hopes of finding a mutual resolution. So, when someone hurts my feelings I will instead describe how I feel instead of saying "you did this or that." It also helps to keep an open mind in case there are things that we need to work on to resolve the situation amicably. This goes back to our intentions when communicating. Do I want to be heard, be right or be effective?

Be an active listener

Once it was pointed out to me that I wasn't being an active listener I set out to work on it. So, now when others are talking I listen intently instead of thinking about my response. This means that I have to make it okay to not have a clever response ready as soon as the other person is done talking. However, we shouldn't be so busy that we have to rush through any of our conversations in such a way that it leaves the other party feeling disrespected. This is just another opportunity for me to practice patience and mindfulness. Now, I try to stay present in the moment when listening and give the speaker my full attention. This takes a lot of the pressure off of me and helps me to be more relaxed in my conversations.

Use your words to uplift others

As the old adage goes "if you don't have something nice to say then don't say anything at all." I try to follow this rule because if someone is having a hard time then talking bad about that person does nothing to improve the situation. Gossip has no place in our homes and communities and only serves to disrupt our balance. I mentioned before that I was a drama hound because I lived in chaos and drama for so many years but you can break that cycle. When we refuse to participate in gossip and only use our words to uplift one another then we give others permission to do the same. Where before I would be tempted to gossip about someone I will now pray for that person who is having a hard time. I know I wouldn't want others talking bad about me when I was struggling. Everyone is doing the best that they can and many people are fighting battles that we know nothing about, so practicing empathy and compassion helps to restore balance.

Self-Care

ᎣᏩᏌ-ᎠᏓᎦᏎᏍᏙᏗ
Owasa-adagasesdodi

We aspire to practice self-care regularly despite our busy schedules.

Traditionally, Cherokee people placed a high value on self-care and understood that it directly impacts our health. Ultimately, we are responsible for our own well-being and the better that we care for ourselves the better we will feel. If we can practice self-care regularly then we will also be able to better care for others. Sadly, self-care seems to be valued less and less as we are expected to be more productive. However, when we take the time and make self-care a priority we actually increase our productivity because we feel better and operate at a higher level of efficiency. Our idea of self-care will differ from person to person but it pretty much just means what you do to care for yourself. With all of the responsibilities of school, work, social life, family obligations, sports and other demands on our time, how do you recharge your batteries?

I was reminded once not to "burn the candle at both ends" because I was trying to juggle school, work and other obligations without taking time to rest and recuperate. Long story short, I did not do very well in any area because I was trying to juggle too much and I did a lot for others without taking care of myself. So, now I make sure to take time for myself and I protect that time. It seems that self-care is usually the first thing to get dismissed when we are in a bind but it is important not to do that. Learning to say "no" has helped me preserve my self-care time and make sure that I am not over-extending myself. So, now I make sure that I take time throughout the day to practice self-care and relax. Though I focus on living a healthy lifestyle I will also have days where I sleep late and eat my favorite comfort food. "All things in moderation, including moderation" as the saying goes. We can either take time for our wellness or we may end up being forced to make time for illness.

Taking the time to practice self-care is not easy and it takes practice to create space for yourself without feeling selfish. For those who have a lot of responsibilities and commitments, this can take some getting used to but the benefits will be measurable. When I was young I was told that I needed to take care of myself before I tried to take care of other people. Surprise! I didn't listen and instead chose to run on self-will and caffeine thinking this is what being an adult was all about. A lot of us have seen the cats in the cradle scenario play out where we model ourselves after our parents and take little time for anything besides work. Of course, work is important. Education is important. Passion is important. However, self-care is also important and I have found that the more time that I take for my self-care then the more energy I have for those I love and for my work. When I am taking care of myself regularly then I feel balanced and strong and patient.

While it is hard to find time to practice self-care it really doesn't require much time at all. It can be as simple as a 5-minute meditation in the morning. A solo run to Starbucks while you sing along to your favorite music. A ten-minute walk on your break or a 20-minute yoga routine at lunch. Our self-care can be whatever we want and as long as we want. Whatever helps to reduce stress in your life and helps you to refocus toward the positive. I know there are moms out there who may be rolling their eyes right now because a lot of times it is hard for moms to find time to shower or use the restroom without the entire house knocking on the door because they need something. I feel you. However, if we can schedule small amounts of time for our self-care then the whole house will be better off for it. This may require us to use our effective communication skills to assertively let people know what we need. It may require others in the house to contribute more and it may require some scheduling but it is possible. Each of us are powerful and we can accomplish anything that we set our mind to so scheduling and practicing self-care is possible.

For us to be able to practice self-care regularly, we first have to change the way that we think about our health. I know that we have gone for so long living with high amounts of stress and anxiety that we are now used to it. So why change right? Well, there is more and more research now that shows how stress and anxiety can make us more prone to illness and could actually shorten our lives. Not to mention the fact that we will not enjoy our lives as much if we do not feel well. So, while practicing self-care regularly will have immediate effects, it will also help us to live a longer, healthier and more fulfilled life. So, now that we know why we should do it the next thing we have to do is set an intention to practice self-care regularly despite our busy schedules.

As we are aware of the benefits of practicing self-care we now also have to accept what may be an uncomfortable truth for some. We deserve to feel good and we deserve time for ourselves. I know that this notion seems quite simple but a lot of people feel guilty for putting themselves first, myself included. For us to change the way that we view our own needs we can pull out the teachings around self-compassion and put the same amount of energy into ourselves that we do our children, spouses and friends. Yes, I care about and want to help others but I have to first care for and help myself. I remember a magnet I saw on someone's fridge that said "If momma ain't happy ain't nobody happy." That pretty much sums up how self-care works to improve the lives of those around us because when I take time for myself then I have more energy and patience for those around me. If you are still struggling with the belief that you are worthy of self-care and feeling better then positive affirmations are helpful to speak this idea into existence. You can say it every time you wash your hands. "I love myself and deserve to feel good." "I am worthy and deserving of my self-care time." "My body and mind work hard for my family and deserves love and care." Say it until you believe it because it is true.

Now that we are working toward believing that we deserve to feel good we can set an intention to practice self-care. Once I made the decision to practice self-care I couldn't just say it once, I had to remind myself every day. So, in the morning, I would just sit quietly and set my intentions for the day. One of my intentions is "I will practice self-care despite my busy schedule." Setting that intention really helps me to sharpen my focus and make sure that my self-care stays a priority because life happens and it is really easy to stop taking care of ourselves if we are not reminded to do so. Another good way to ensure that you make time for self-care is to schedule your self-care activities or routine. I write my self-care activities in my calendar book that way I know if I am available when other projects require my time. Unless it is an emergency I can almost always make sure that I get to both take care of others and take care of myself as well. Once I have my self-care activities written down I make sure to protect that time and will say "no" to others if there is a scheduling conflict.

When I schedule my self-care time I am not talking about a huge part of my day. For me it looks like a three-minute meditation after coffee, doing my gratitude list in the shower, doing positive affirmations when I wash my hands, walking or doing a twenty-minute yoga routine at lunch. Eating healthy is also a part of my self-care along with making sure I attend my mental health and physical health appointments. However, my self-care routine also has to be enjoyable or I know that I will not stick to it. So, I make sure to schedule activities that I like doing and are realistic. For example, I have tried my whole life to be a gym guy as I wanted to be physically fit and have a lot of muscles. However, I hated the whole gym routine. First I had to shower (don't ask me as I am still not sure why). Then I got dressed and had to drive to the gym where I would often have to wait for a machine, then worked out and drove back home for another shower. Needless to say that since I did not really enjoy the whole process at all I wouldn't stick with the routine at all and would just be left with a gym membership that I did not use. I really like working out at home or in the office or taking walks. My fitness routine now consists of yoga and various calisthenics, walking or running on my treadmill and using dumbbells. This may not be your cup of tea but I enjoy it a lot more than going to the gym so I stick with it and my fitness routine really makes me feel better.

Action Steps

Gratitude exercises

Practicing gratitude every day is an important part of my self-care. This helps me to focus on what is good in life instead of worrying and stressing about things. This helps to keep my thoughts focused on the positive which keeps me moving forward in the right direction. I also find that practicing gratitude makes me excited about life and gives me energy. I say several prayers throughout the day to give thanks, I do a gratitude list in the shower in the morning and I tell others in my life that I am grateful for them.

Positive affirmations

Positive affirmations are another part of my self-care routine that helps me to love and accept myself every day. Making these activities a part of my self-care routine ensures that I do them every day instead of just when I do not feel good. I am quite proud of myself for being proactive because in the past I had a habit of quitting on self-care once I felt better but this just ensured that my progress would be short-lived. Now I practice positive affirmations every time I wash my hands and it continues to improve my self-acceptance and self-confidence.

Follow through with doctor appointments & mental health appointments

In the past, I often would avoid the doctor because I didn't want to hear any bad news. However, that didn't make any sense because if I was ill then my avoiding the doctor only served to make my condition worse and delay the inevitable news. So, now I go to all of my doctor appointments and follow-ups so that any issue can be detected and treated early. I also make sure to attend my mental health appointments because mental health is just as important as physical health. I am grateful to be able to access resources to help me process life's ups and downs.

Take time to rest

No matter how well you take care of yourself life can still be exhausting at times. A lot is expected of us and we must take time to recharge our batteries. Sleep is important but rest is equally important.

How we rest may differ from person to person, for instance, I feel rested after doing yoga while you may prefer watching Netflix. How we practice it is personal but the need for it is universal. So, whether it means closing your eyes for a few minutes on your breaks or sitting outside in nature, it will help us to set aside time to rest.

Say "no" for self-care

I have learned that I cannot expect others to put my needs and health first. I am responsible for ensuring that I am well and that means that I have to make sure that I make my self-care a priority. I cannot blame others for asking for help because they have their own needs in mind and I am happy to be of service. However, if I need rest then I have to decline invites from time to time and if someone needs help during one of my scheduled self-care activities then I will say "no" or reschedule. When I am rested then I feel better and am actually more productive and helpful.

Eat healthy & exercise

Eating healthy and exercising for self-care means that we do it regularly as a part of our self-care routine. What has helped me is to make things simple and make small adjustments to my regular routine. If your healthy habits are manageable then you are more likely to stick with them and find sustained success. I quit drinking soda (pop to Midwesterners), exercise daily and eat a balanced diet. However, I did not attempt to do it all at once but made small changes over time.

Do things just for fun

I can sometimes overlook this component of self-care but it is equally important. Life is meant to be enjoyed and finding those things that make us smile and laugh are important and promote gratitude. Cherokee people understood that we are not meant to always be productive. Playing stickball where we laugh and run and play is actually a part of our ceremonial life. Such is the importance placed on joy in our lives.

Time management

I for one know firsthand how poor time management can increase stress and anxiety. I always seemed to be late for something and my to-do list only got longer. Of course, traditionally we weren't so pressed for time but now we are often pulled in several different directions so better time management has proven beneficial. What made this easier for me was prioritizing my time. I had to accept that I can't be everywhere at once and so I had to choose where I placed my focus and energy. It also helped me to prioritize things based on when they needed to be done. So once I knew what my priorities were I could then make a manageable schedule based around my self-care so I knew when I could say "yes" to others or politely decline.

Perseverance

ᏗᏓᏲᎯᏍᏗ ᏂᎨᏒᎾ
Didayohisdi nigesvna

We aspire to persevere despite any challenge that comes our way.

My aunt Wilma Mankiller, who is a former Chief of the Cherokee Nation, best summed up the perseverance of Cherokee people when she said, "The secret of our success is that we never, never give up." Despite facing extreme adversity for hundreds of years, Cherokee people have been able to persevere because we keep moving forward no matter what. I think of this often when my fear of failure creeps in and tries to talk me out of taking a healthy risk. "Well, what if I fail?" I ask myself. So what. Every time I fail at something I always learn a lot and then the next time I try I have a better chance of success. Instead of thinking about worst-case scenarios now I try and think "what's the best that could happen" and I focus on that. This is my life and I want to live with purpose.

So how do you practice perseverance? Why is it that when things get hard some people shine while others give up? There are several reasons but I believe that it starts with how you prepare for whatever task you are trying to accomplish. As the old saying goes "anything worth doing is worth doing right." Research your interest and see what education or training will help you to be successful. Also, it is very helpful to have a strong support system for when times get tough and you need advice or just someone to talk to. It is also important to be clear about your motivation and to have realistic expectations.

If you are clear about your reasons for doing something then that will help you to maintain focus and see things through to the end. You should also expect some adversity and not let it get you down. Learning new things is hard and practicing self-compassion during tough times will help you to continue with good energy despite any setbacks. Just because something is hard or challenging doesn't mean that it is impossible. Our people have faced extreme adversity but have stayed the course because some adversity is to be expected. That is life. So, when you run into tough times look at the situation as a challenge instead of a problem. Adversity is just an opportunity to learn so take the lesson and learn what you need to from the situation and move on.

Next, it is important to be mindful of how you talk to yourself about the process. If you talk negatively to yourself along the way then it is entirely possible that the stress will eventually become too much and you will quit. However, if you talk to yourself in a positive way and be your own cheerleader then you will move through adversity much easier and will be more likely to succeed. Practicing positive self-talk will also help you to be more patient with the process and will help avoid unnecessary frustration along the way. If something that I am working on doesn't happen right away due to setbacks or adversity then I can pause and reassess my plan. This is a good opportunity to practice patience because even though things may not happen exactly when I want I know that they will eventually happen if I do not give up. So, if you do not get the job or the grade you wanted that is ok. You are on the right road and your hard work will eventually pay off if you believe.

Having faith in ourselves is important if we want to succeed in our endeavors. This does take practice but it is possible for everyone. No matter what situation you are in if you believe in yourself then there isn't anything that you cannot accomplish. We can incorporate this belief into our daily affirmations if need be so that we can be reminded of our power and our resolve. Every time you wash your hands you can say "I am powerful" or "I will accomplish all of my goals" or "everything happens for my highest good." This helped me when I was struggling with self-belief and although I did not believe it in the beginning I just kept saying it over and over until I did.

If we set an intention to persevere then we will. So whatever you are trying to accomplish just know that you will eventually be successful if you keep working toward your goal and do not quit. I know that it is scary to take a healthy risk because there is always a possibility that things will not work out exactly how you planned but that is life. We can either flow with the universe or fight against it. This means that although I set an intention to make a living by helping others I did not picture my current position exactly. As I learned more my course has changed over time and the universe has presented different opportunities than what I imagined I would be doing. Because I like to be in control at all times it was difficult in the beginning to remain open to all possibilities that could change my goals. However, because I stayed the course and did not quit when things got hard or didn't turn out the way I wanted I now have many opportunities that I never imagined. So if doors do not open right away and the change you seek eludes you at first do not lose heart. The positive outcomes you seek will eventually come to fruition if you can persevere through adversity. Things may not turn out exactly how we picture but if we remain open to all possibilities and put in the work, then we will be successful.

Writing this book is a good case in point. I struggled with self-belief at times. I struggled to find the time to write. I struggled with the message I was trying to convey. I became impatient and wanted to procrastinate. I had thoughts that said someone else should publish this knowledge. Who am I to teach this curriculum? What if nobody likes the book? Maybe I should quit and do something else. It could have all ended so easily. Quitting something may seem like a single decision but the process of quitting actually starts way before and begins with how you talk to yourself about the process. In the past, I may have entertained my negative thoughts instead of changing them. It would have been easy to let my frustration convince me to quit so that I wouldn't be uncomfortable anymore. But I didn't quit. When I struggled I remembered my motivation for writing this book in the first place. I wanted to help people. That motivated me through the hard times. Also, doing positive affirmations and practicing positive thinking helped me see that I was just anxious and that was okay. It was okay to struggle and it was okay to start over and over and over again if need be. And what if no one likes the book? Who cares? The Walking In Balance curriculum is helping people right now through virtual classes that I teach and it helps me as well. I didn't quit and I put this information out into the universe just in case someone may find it of use in their journey. To me that is success. I have succeeded. I have persevered and you can too.

So no matter what situation you currently find yourself in just know that you will find success if you put in the work and do not give up. Whether your goals involve sobriety, education, employment, family or self-improvement, success is in your intentions and your journey. You are successful for trying. You are successful for failing. You are successful because you continue to get up, dust yourself off and try again and again and again if needed. That is success in a nutshell and it rarely looks exactly how we envisioned it. However, you are in good company as anyone who has ever pushed themselves would tell you that the work is worth it.

Action Steps

Be clear about motivation

When times get tough it helps me to remember why I started doing something in the first place. Whether my motivation is to better myself or my community it helps to put things into perspective during times of adversity.

Have clear goals that are measurable and attainable

In the past, I would often set myself up for failure because I set goals that were unrealistic and unattainable. After an honest assessment of my skills I now have a better idea of what I can get done and in what time frame.

Break goals down into manageable steps

Once I set my sights on a goal I break the process down into manageable steps. This allows me to not become overwhelmed by the big picture but instead, I can just focus on what I have to do this day or this hour. This also enables me to track my progress and I can rejoice in all of my small accomplishments along the way.

Expect some adversity

For much of my life, I have been a worst-case-scenario kind of guy. I was always hyper-vigilant waiting for the next shoe to drop. I thought that this was helping me to stay prepared but it really just made me exhausted. Now, because I have worked hard on changing my negative thinking and talking to myself more positively, I no longer feel like the sky is falling all of the time. So, while I do expect some adversity in life I get to view it as a challenge instead of a problem. I feel like I have a more accurate and balanced view of the world because I can keep things in perspective. So, when adversity does come my way I see it for the learning experience that it is and I know that I have the skills to meet the challenge. I no longer let a little adversity stop my progress.

Look at challenges as opportunities to grow

As I mentioned before, we get to decide what our lives look like depending on how we talk to ourselves. So when you are faced with challenges you can tell yourself "I can't do this" or "great, why is everything so hard" and stress yourself out. Or you can say "well, that didn't turn out how I wanted but it's not a big deal and I will figure it out." I do this a lot and it helps me to reframe the situation because I look at things in a more positive light now. Where I would whine before and feel sorry for myself I now shake it off and just see how I can accomplish the task and what I need to learn from the process. This has enabled me to continue pushing myself to take healthy risks and continue to grow.

Ask for help

Asking for help continues to be one of the best ways to overcome adversity and accomplish my goals. I used to think that I was supposed to know everything but now I realize that I will continue learning for the rest of my life which is pretty awesome. I know only a little and that is okay because I do not have to be good at everything. I have my talents and when I need assistance I get to draw on someone else's talents and knowledge in order to accomplish my goals. It is humbling to ask for help but humility is a good thing. I feel like this is why everyone is given different talents and experiences so that we can come together and help each other when times get tough. I was often scared to ask for help in the past but I have never been turned down when I was sincere and asked someone for help.

Be your own cheerleader

Practicing self-compassion really helps me when facing adversity. For many years I wouldn't follow through with something unless I knew that everything would go perfectly and I missed out on a lot of opportunities because of it. Now I am happy that my self-worth is not dictated by how others see me but by effort. So, as long as I am giving it my all then I am no longer concerned with how things turn out. If things turn out well then that is great, however, if things do not turn out well then that is just an opportunity to learn instead of an opportunity to be self-critical. I remind myself often that I am proud of the work that I am doing and that I am proud of my effort. This helps me to keep things in perspective because I measure my success based on how far I have come instead of comparing myself to others. Saying positive affirmations daily helps me to frame my efforts in a positive light.

Service

ᎢᏓᏛᏁᏗ
Idadvnedi

We aspire to be of service to others whenever possible and help each other Walk In Balance.

Now more than ever we need to lift one another up whenever possible and practice compassion through service. If we practiced compassion more the world would be a better place with more opportunities for all. Showing compassion towards others promotes connection and helps us to see things from other's perspectives. Practicing compassion puts our empathy for others into motion and enables us to work for each other. The Cherokee word for this is Gadugi which means working together and it is compassion put into action. This is one of the reasons that Cherokee people have survived in the face of extreme hardship throughout the years. After removal and the Trail of Tears, Cherokee people found themselves in a new land with very limited resources. When Cherokee people were forced to leave their homelands in the east and walk to what is now Oklahoma they often were only allowed to take what they could carry. I cannot imagine what they felt as they were forced from their homeland with many people passing away on the journey. In our cultural teachings, Cherokee people are taught not to worry but to work for each other and that is what they did and have continued to do since then.

Another example of Gadugi that comes to mind is the Bell Water Project. My aunt Wilma Mankiller organized the community of Bell, Oklahoma in the early '80s and helped them complete a very ambitious task of providing running water to the community. Many residents in the community did not have indoor plumbing or running water so Wilma identified resources for the project and organized the community. The residents performed the self-improvement work themselves and finished a 16-mile waterline for the community. The Bell Water Project was a monumental achievement and continues to serve as a wonderful example of how service to others can change lives.

It isn't just big service projects that are important, however, small everyday gestures can vastly improve the lives of those around us as well as our own. My spiritual sister Cynthia Ruiz often reminds me of a quote by Maya Angelou. "I've learned that people will forget what you said, people will forget what you did, but people will never forget how you made them feel." This quote illustrates the importance of practicing compassion and being of service to others. One of the ways that

Cynthia has been of service is by mentoring others, myself included. Cynthia's mentorship of myself and others demonstrates how compassion can change our world for the better. To me, compassion means caring for someone so much that you are motivated to help them. It is important to show compassion to others and to yourself as well. As a man, I believe that showing compassion is a sign of strength. Some may see compassion as a weakness but it takes strength to care so much that you are inspired to act.

Being of service to others provides many benefits. The first benefit is that it feels good to help others. One of the best ways to get yourself out of a funk is to be of service and help someone. Whether you are helping out in your house by doing the dishes, cleaning a neighbor's yard or volunteering in your community, it just feels good to help others. Putting a smile on someone's face can put a smile on yours as well. This is because being of service to others affirms gratitude for our blessings and puts that gratitude into action. When we perform service for others we can balance out all that we have received from the universe. Some people refer to this as karma or paying it forward but it is important to give to the universe to balance out what we take from the universe. This helps us to live in balance. Cherokee people are taught this when they harvest anything from nature whether it is animal or plant. We leave an offering or item to balance out what we consume. For instance, if I go out to harvest a plant for medicinal purposes then I may water the plant that I harvested from. I will also say a prayer and give thanks for what I was able to harvest.

Another benefit of service is that we improve the communities and world in which we live. Everyone wants to live in a healthy and peaceful community and one way that we can help make that happen is through service. I've heard it said many times that "we are only as strong as our weakest link." I believe that our success as a community is not demonstrated by who has the most but by how we support those who have the least. In Cherokee culture, we are taught to help others because that is the right thing to do. Cherokees have always practiced servant leadership and we expect our leaders to serve. This ensures that we stay connected to our communities and do not lose sight of what is important.

Service promotes connection in our households and communities and helps us to feel more fulfilled. Money cannot buy you happiness but being of service can help you to feel more grateful, fulfilled and joyful. So, find a way to give back to your community and household in a way that fits your lifestyle and schedule. This will make it more likely that you will continue to give back on a regular basis. If possible I pick household chores that I am good at like cleaning the bathroom. Many people might not like this chore but I don't mind it and it makes me happy knowing that I am contributing to our household. There are also many ways to give back to your community such as volunteering, donating money or mentoring others. Give back in a way that promotes your values and well-being. If we give too much of ourselves then we may end up depleted and then we are no good to anybody. We cannot be everything to everyone. Do not let yourself feel pressured to do everything. Just do your part. You have been blessed with unique talents so use those talents to make the world a better place. Be good to others and yourself as well.

Action Steps

Thinking of and praying for others

Even though I aim to be of service to others daily, I actually begin thinking of other people early on in my day. Right after I do my gratitude list in the morning I list 3 or 4 things that I want for others. I believe that wanting things for others or praying for others sends good energy their way and is beneficial for you as well because it helps us to feel more connected to our loved ones.

Ask how you can help

One of the greatest gifts of working the Walking In Balance program is that I have a lot more energy and empathy for others. So, if I see someone who needs some help I can reach out and ask that person what I can do for them. I believe that this is another way for us to maintain balance in our lives and in our communities. So, if you see someone who is struggling do not be shy about reaching out.

Be of service in your household

Being of service in our households helps to maintain balance because it helps if all of the responsibility isn't just on one or two people. So, find a way to contribute to your household whether through chores or other ways because it not only helps lighten the load for others but it is a great way to express gratitude.

Be of service in your community

The same concept of balance can be applied to our communities. I have often passed a field or waterway that was littered with trash and thought to myself "someone should do something about that" but what if that someone is me? It takes a minimal amount of time to pick up a bag of trash and it feels really good to be of service in my community. I think that we often become complacent because the idea of property "ownership" has left us feeling like a bunch of individuals instead of a community. However, this is not a Cherokee value because we believe that we all belong to the land and are all related. So, I often look for different opportunities to volunteer and be of service in my community as a way to show that I care and to help maintain balance.

Be of service in a way that fits your lifestyle

I mentioned before that one of the things that I love about the Walking In Balance program is that everyone gets to practice it in their own way and service is no different. What works for me and my schedule may not work for you so don't feel bad if you do not have time to volunteer or mentor others right now. However, maybe you have resources to donate to causes in your community. Being of service in a way that fits your lifestyle is compassion put into action and enables us to express our gratitude for all that we are blessed with.

Balance

ᎢᎦᏗᎭᏊ
Igatihaquu

We aspire to Walk In Balance with our spirit and environment.

One of the best examples of how to Walk In Balance was my aunt Wilma Mankiller who often said that "every day is a good day." I used one of her quotes in the section on Perseverance but I could share stories about her on every topic as she is the perfect example of how to Walk In Balance. She persevered despite facing adversity that would overwhelm many and made it look easy. She graduated college despite being a single parent of two young children and later became the first female Principal Chief of the Cherokee Nation where she endured much harassment because of her gender. She often said that she experienced more prejudice because of her gender than her race which is striking because Cherokee society is historically matriarchal. During her tenure, she was able to accomplish a lot for Cherokee people and never became resentful of others despite many efforts to thwart her agenda and threaten her into silence. A lot of bad things were said about her just because she was a woman but she never let it distract her from her goals. She once told me "people are going to talk about you no matter what you do so you might as well do what you want."

It wasn't only in the political arena where Wilma faced adversity, however. She was involved in a devastating car crash as an adult that caused significant injuries and took the life of one of her friends. She also suffered from polycystic kidney disease and had to endure two kidney transplants as well as battle cancer and other health issues. I believe that she was able to persevere through trials that would sideline many because of her positive outlook and her ability to Walk In Balance. She embodied everything that Cherokee culture and the Walking In Balance program aspires to teach and is a huge inspiration of mine. I remember when I was a kid just looking at her in awe because of what she accomplished despite her troubles and she did it often with a smile on her face. Like many Cherokee people, she had a great sense of humor and laughed often despite her pain. She was able to practice every component of the Walking in Balance curriculum and it enabled her to "live her best life." Now we get to follow her example and others who have come before us so that we may also live a fulfilled life of wellness. The goal is to live in a way so that when we are done we can be proud of what we accomplished and not carry the burden of regret. So how do we balance all of these different aspects of wellness and incorporate them into our already busy lives?

By following Aunt Wilma's example I believe the key is to not let ourselves get pulled away from our center. We must stay connected in order to fulfill our spiritual purpose. For me, this means that I practice all of the components of the Walking In Balance program regularly. It means that I have an action plan where I schedule my wellness activities and self-care and I protect that time. I also practice self-compassion and when life happens and I get off course a little then I give myself permission to not be perfect instead of trying to overcompensate. There is a saying in Alcoholics Anonymous. "Progress not perfection." I like that saying because it allows us to get better without the unrealistic expectation that we will get it right all the time. Yes, we do the work but then take time to enjoy our lives and we trust that the universe is working on our behalf.

How I maintain balance in my life is that I put my wellness first. This is a difficult concept for many, especially parents and those who take care of others but it is important. If I am not taking care of myself then I may not have the energy to take care of others. Pretty simple. Next, I make sure that I schedule my wellness activities and I stick to the schedule the best I can. Your schedule may look different than mine but I schedule activities that address my physical, mental, emotional, social and spiritual wellness as well as activities just for fun. These activities do not have to be long in duration or effort either. The point is that we balance our wellness with our other responsibilities like work and family. When I am balanced in my wellness program then I enjoy myself more at work and with my family. I am more present, attentive and compassionate toward others. Balance ensures that we can have it all. Family, success, happiness and love are all possible if we can maintain balance in our lives for the most part. I say for the most part because I know life happens and you may get out of balance at times but that is entirely okay. When we have tough times or are forced out of our routine for a bit then we get to practice self-compassion and ease ourselves back into our program and keep moving forward.

Action Steps

Define what balance means to you

Everyone's needs and schedules are different so you get to determine what balance looks like in your life. You may start by asking yourself what fulfillment looks like to you. For me it means that for the most part, I am eating healthy, I am exercising regularly and I practice gratitude and positive thinking regularly. It also helps me to practice mindfulness, wellness and self-compassion. When I am balanced in my life through these self-care activities then I feel balanced at work, at home and in my community. I can work without bringing it home, I can be present for my family and I have the energy to be of service in my community.

Schedule your wellness activities and protect that time

It continues to help me stay organized and on track when I schedule my wellness activities. This is because life can get so busy so fast and it will be your self-care that is the first thing to get overlooked in a pinch. This is because we care a lot for others and have a tendency to put our well-being last when life gets busy. So, by scheduling your wellness activities you can stay on track and it will stay in balance because you will know whether or not you have time for other commitments.

Practice self-compassion

I work hard to live my life in a balanced way but it is hard in our society. A lot is expected out of us and our children so it is easy to get out of balance or forget to take care of yourself. When this happens you may be tempted to get down on yourself for not sticking with your wellness activities but it does not help for us to be self-critical. Instead, I practice self-compassion and I let myself know that it is okay. I am still doing great and it is not a big deal to get off track sometimes. I can just get right back on track and keep moving forward. This helps me much more than getting down on myself and I recover much quicker. You all are doing the best you can and life is hard sometimes so be a friend to yourself. Forgive yourself and talk to yourself in a good way. You deserve it.

Do not overcompensate in any one area

If I do miss a workout or something the tendency is to go extra hard the next day but that is detrimental to our balance. It doesn't help for us to exhaust ourselves just because we had to take a day off. Maybe you don't feel well and need a nap instead of a workout, maybe you need some support from others. Whatever the case do not feel bad if you are not perfect in all of your endeavors. None of us are. We do the best we can and that is enough.

Action

ᎠᎵᏖᎸᏂᏓᏍᏗ
Alitelvnidasdi

We aspire to accomplish our goals through action and personal responsibility.

Cherokees have always believed that each of us is personally responsible for our own wellness. As with anything in life, you get out what you put in. The Walking In Balance program is no different. If I do not put in the work then I may lose my spiritual connection, lose respect for myself, run on self-will and be overcome with stress and anxiety. However, when I do put in the work then I feel connected, balanced, loved, loving and peaceful. Because we are often being pulled in several directions at once it is helpful for us to schedule our Walking In Balance activities. Inevitably, life gets busy and when it does it seems as though our self-care and personal development activities are the first things to fall by the wayside. I find it easier if I incorporate many of the action steps into my existing routine so that it just becomes a habit. For instance, I do positive affirmations every time I wash my hands and do my gratitude list every morning while showering.

I know this seems like a lot to worry about but it is pretty simple to incorporate into your day. For instance, a typical day for me starts with waking up and thanking the Creator for another day on this earth. Then, as I mentioned before, while I shower I list things that I am grateful for and also some things that I want for others. Sometimes my gratitude list is short and sometimes I am still listing things after my shower is done. The point is that I focus on all of the good things in my life instead of worrying about what I don't have. Next, when I braid my hair or my spouse braids my hair I set an intention for my day and think about the positive outcomes that I want for myself and others.

I have made a commitment to healthy eating and I always say a quick prayer before I eat because I am very thankful for the food that I have. During the pandemic, it was suggested that we sing happy birthday twice in our head while washing our hands but I decided to take that time and say positive affirmations instead because I have struggled with that in the past. On my breaks in my office, I do yoga or other aerobic exercises and on my lunch break, I take a walk or jog. I make sure to stay connected to others and I have healthy boundaries that enable me to only have supportive people in my life. If

I find myself annoyed or irritable then I take a minute to check in with my feelings and emotions to determine the cause so that I can process them. I also communicate my feelings with others and practice active listening. I make sure to go to all mental and physical health appointments as that helps me to maintain my wellness. I then end my day by doing a "what went well" list so that I can focus on what I did well instead of expectations that I may not have met. I then spend time with my family and watch a little TV or read then I say one more prayer to give thanks for the day I was able to have and it is time to get a good night's rest.

I am not able to stick to my routine 100% of the time. Life happens. However, if we make the choice to live a life of wellness and are on the right road then we will have many more good days than bad. I have a daily, weekly and monthly routine that enables me to put the program into action. There are some activities that I do daily like practicing gratitude, physical activity, mindfulness and positive affirmations. While other activities I may do weekly like going to my counseling sessions, performing community service and activities that promote spiritual wellness. Then there are action steps that are bi-weekly or monthly like going to medical checkups, date nights with my spouse and going to a Stomp Dance.

How you practice each component of the Walking In Balance curriculum is up to you. I have outlined how I have implemented the program into my life and have given some examples but you get to decide how you want to work the program. Everyone's life is different and I believe a personalized action plan is very helpful because it is easier to stick with things that you enjoy doing. I love walking and playing stickball for physical activity while you may enjoy running and lifting weights. I practice mindfulness by doing yoga or crafting while you may prefer guided meditation. The point is that we take action in order to live a life of wellness. Ultimately, we are responsible for our own health and well-being and it will help to have a wellness program that we enjoy. I feel like the internet was created for this sort of program that should be tailored to the individual. All you have to do is Google "how to practice mindfulness" and you can find different suggestions on how to implement mindfulness into your life.

Maybe you would like to incorporate a little of each component into your daily or weekly schedule or perhaps focus on one of the teachings. Either way, as long as you are balanced in your daily routine then you should see a marked improvement in whatever area you are working on. When you take action then you are affirming that you are in control of your life and no one else. When we do not take action then we leave a lot to chance and often end up with anxiety and stress. So make your wellness and self-care appointments. Get your checkups, see a counselor if you want, get your hair done and do something just for fun. If we do not make the time for our wellness then eventually our health will decline to the point that we are forced to make time.

We can no longer use the excuse that "we do not have the time" for our wellness. We have loads of time but we just prioritize other things ahead of our wellness. I get it though. Between work and education and family, there seems to not be enough hours in the day sometimes. However, if we prioritize our wellness and incorporate a balanced schedule of activities then we will actually be more productive and will feel better as well. Remember that you can say "no." You do not have to feel bad. If someone needs you to do something and it is during one of your self-care activity times then just say "I can help you tomorrow but I am busy today." We cannot count on others to put us first so our wellness should be our first priority. It also helps to have an action plan for your daily routine and an action plan for when you are triggered by stress or loss. This doesn't take much time but it can have a profound impact on your ability to cope with stressful situations.

Action Steps

Identify goals of the action plan

When we are creating our action plan it is important to identify what we want to accomplish. Since I am a visual person I will write my goals down so that I can see them often and be reminded of why I am putting in the work. For instance, if you want to increase your feelings of gratitude then you might schedule a daily gratitude exercise.

Make a realistic action plan

My mother often told me that my eyes were too big for my stomach. She was right and that is something that I have had to work on to have sustained success in any area. I would often set lofty goals for myself that were unrealistic and would inevitably end in failure. I always thought that my failure was due to a lack of effort but it was instead due to a lack of planning. When you set your goals make sure that you take into account your other obligations and it is important to recognize that you only have so much energy. As you get older you may find that you have less and less energy so it is important to prioritize your tasks. It helps me to stick with things that I enjoy doing so try to find wellness activities that fit into your lifestyle. Try not to do everything at once. It may be helpful to pick one component per week to incorporate into your daily living.

Incorporate Walking In Balance activities into existing habits

I know that life moves fast and it is very easy to get overwhelmed. When this happens it seems like our self-care is the first thing to go out the window. So, I try to schedule self-care activities at regular intervals that I will remember. For instance, I do my gratitude list every day while in the shower and do positive affirmations every time I wash my hands. I do yoga on my first break and take a walk every day on my lunch break. I also do my "what went well" list every night when I brush my teeth. These are just a few examples of how you can incorporate self-care activities into your existing habits which may help you to remember them.

Periodically evaluate your action plan

Due to our experiences, we continue to change and evolve. Our schedules also may need to change from time to time so it is beneficial to reevaluate your action plan. This will help you to stay organized and balanced which will lead to more sustained success.

Have a plan for emergencies

Unfortunately, we all will experience hardship and loss. This was made evident by the pandemic but it will help us to continue to move forward positively if we have a plan for those times. It doesn't have to be anything complicated either. Just a list of supportive people to call, mental health resources to take advantage of, or a few coping skills to practice when stressed. Though it may not seem like much, having a list of resources and coping skills can go a long way toward helping you cope when facing adversity or loss.

Walking In Balance

Frankly, it is not my family's responsibility to make me happy. It is my own. When I am balanced and actively participating in my wellness regimen then I am happy and we get to be happy together. You know what you need better than anyone else so create an action plan that addresses your needs and do what you enjoy. You know if you need to stop drinking, you know if you need to practice positive thinking and you know what you enjoy doing for self-care. So, do not be afraid to take the healthy risk and ask for help if needed. Be brave.

Made in the USA
Monee, IL
18 June 2024

59585761R00118